ON WHAT IS LEARNED

IN

ROBERT DREEBEN

HARVARD UNIVERSITY

ADDISON-WESLEY PUBLISHING COMPANY
Reading, Massachusetts
Ontario

This book is in the

ADDISON-WESLEY SERIES IN EDUCATION
Social, Behavioral, and Philosophical Foundations

Byron G. Massialas, Series Editor

FOREWORD

This series is designed primarily for those who will assume leadership roles in the schools of today—the teachers. In a rapidly changing world, schools are required to develop new educational roles and perspectives; more than ever before they pay attention, directly or indirectly, to the social, political, and economic conditions of the larger society. In this new era, education is considered to be an investment in national development, and equalitarian principles increasingly provide the basis for educational policies. Such factors as the socioeconomic status of children, their ethnicity, regional differences, occupational aspirations, and their beliefs and values have been gaining in importance. These and similar factors determine to a large extent the educational environment needed to generate in children a motivation to learn, to think critically, and to develop defensible ideas about themselves and society.

Consciously or unconsciously, teachers impart norms of the individual's role in society. Regardless of their subject of instruction, teachers have, for example, the potential for performing a political socialization function—they are in a position to convey to children knowledge about and attitudes toward the political system. Children begin, at a very young age, to internalize the political norms which characterize the system; e.g., participation, social trust, political efficacy, etc.

It is our firm belief that an effective teacher should become thoroughly familiar both with the substantive content of certain of these topics and issues and with the role of the school in dealing effectively with emerging social problems. In turn, the teacher's role is not only to introduce these topics and issues in the context of civilization's past wisdom, but to motivate the student to seek new viewpoints and solutions through his own inquiry skills and creative talents. It is not presumptuous to reaffirm that mankind's future largely depends on the quantity and quality of education of our youth.

Specifically, the books in this series are designed to help the reader understand the following:

1. The functions of education as a social agency and its interrelations with other social agencies.

2. The historical roles of schools and changes in these roles mainly resulting from urbanization and industrialization.

3. The role of education both as an institution and as a process, as it affects personality formation, socialization, cognitive development, and self-concept of the individual.

4. The impact of education on the social, economic, political, and intellectual development of a nation.

5. The influence of education on human values—their formation, justification, adjudication.

In connection with the above, the series attempts to indicate how knowledge-claims in the field have evolved and what particular skills and procedures of social research have been used. The focus is on selected unifying concepts, e.g., socialization, culture diffusion, elite formation, human values, and economic and political modernization as they relate to education. Each volume singles out an aspect of the relation between education and society and deals with it in depth. Each author, while looking at his topic from the perspective of a scholarly discipline, be it history, political science, sociology, or philosophy, tries to draw from other related fields as well.

We hope that these volumes will offer educators and teachers new insights into our understanding of education and the emerging world culture, and that they will open new doors for additional work and study in the social, philosophical, and behavioral foundations of education.

Byron G. Massialas

PREFACE

This book inquires into the nature of schools and the schooling process. It is really a speculative essay designed more to argue a case than to prove, by marshalling evidence and testing hypotheses, that something is so. The perspective is sociological in the sense that it concerns characteristics of the social organization of schools and the experiences of children (who are the participants in schools), insofar as they are shaped by those characteristics. The perspective is also psychological in the sense that it concerns outcomes of the schooling process that are states of mind.

There is an ironical association between our familiarity with schools and our ignorance about them. It is fair to say that no adequate description or formulation of their structural characteristics currently exists, perhaps because the schooling process so obviously involves psychological change that the most reasonable way to study it—or so it would seem—is to look for those psychological changes that appear related to the main business of the school, which is instruction. But surely there is more to schools and schooling than this. The most striking characteristics of school organization reveal themselves when the schooling process is viewed in the context of a developmental sequence that begins with young children as almost completely dependent members of a family, and ends—if it can be said to end—with adults participating in the public arenas of work and politics, a sequence that proceeds through a series of institutional settings, each with characteristic structural properties.

The whole developmental sequence is commonly known as socialization, and schooling represents but one part of it. The total process is a topic far beyond the scope of this book, and in view of that I have placed rather arbitrary boundaries around my argument. I am concerned primarily with formal schooling, but since schools have crucial linkages with other institutions at separated stages of the life cycle, and the character of the schooling process is shaped significantly by the nature of those institutions, I have chosen to anchor my discussion accordingly. I shall be speaking, then, of the family, of elementary and secondary schools, of the occupational sector of the economy, and of the polity. I might well have discussed college as part of the process of formal education, as well as a whole array of other agencies whose contributions are undeniable—adolescent peer groups, the mass media, the armed forces, youth groups, and the like—but to do so would have radically changed the character of this book.

My debts, intellectual and otherwise, are large and go back like the tributaries of a stream. Among the largest is that to Talcott

Parsons, whose influence appears in many pages of this book. Neal Gross, Alex Inkeles, Daniel Levinson, and Elliot Mishler have all, in diverse ways, influenced my thinking on the problems of linking social structure and personality.

In the most immediate sense, four people contributed immeasurably to this book: Barrie Bortnick, Andrew Effrat, Michael Katz, and Larry Weiss. They were colleagues of the best kind: hard to please, liberal with their thoughts, delightfully irreverent. The ideas expressed here are far better for their having sat around a table with me for a year, and I learned much from them.

Charles Bidwell, Neal Gross, and Alex Inkeles gave me careful readings of earlier drafts, which I appreciate greatly. Jeanne Klein and Helen Steinberg helped me by reducing substantial amounts of literature to manageable proportions, for which I express my thanks. My thanks go also to Marion Crowley for her help in typing the final manuscript, to Theresa Kovich and Daniel Woods for their help with proofreading, and to Paul Smith, who took on the tedious task of preparing the index.

With patience, hard work, graciousness, and good spirit, Charlene Worth really got this book out. My debt to her is very great indeed.

I would like to express my gratitude here to the Harvard Center for Research and Development in Educational Differences, directed by Dean Theodore Sizer and John Herzog of the Harvard Graduate School of Education, whose award of a generous grant enabled me to carry out my project on social structure and personality change of which this study is a part.

Cambridge, Massachusetts   R. D.
March, 1968

ACKNOWLEDGMENTS

The research on which this book is based was supported by funds provided through a contract (OE 5-10-239) with the United States Department of Health, Education, and Welfare, Office of Education, under the provisions of the Cooperative Research Program, as a project of the Harvard University Center for Research and Development on Educational Differences. Acknowledgment is gratefully made to the following publishers, who have granted permission to reprint excerpts from copyrighted publications:

The Free Press of Glencoe: Edward C. Banfield, *The Moral Basis of a Backward Society* (1967), and Daniel Lerner, *The Passing of Traditional Society* (1958).

Alfred A. Knopf: Philippe Aries, *Centuries of Childhood*, translated by Robert Baldick (1962).

Random House: Jules Henry, *Culture Against Man* (1963).

Row, Peterson: Philip Selznick, *Leadership in Administration* (1957).

The Canadian Journal of Economics and Political Science: Kaspar D. Naegele, "Clergymen, Teachers, and Psychiatrists: A Study in Roles and Socialization," **22,** No. 1 (1956).

Doubleday: T. H. Marshall, *Class, Citizenship, and Social Development* (1963).

Rand McNally: Arthur L. Stinchcombe, "Social Structure and Organizations," in James G. March (ed.), *Handbook of Organizations* (1965).

Washington University Press: Louis Hartz, "Democracy: Image and Reality," in William N. Chambers and Robert H. Salisbury (eds.), *Democracy in the Mid-Twentieth Century* (1960).

CONTENTS

For my children, Jane, Jill, and Tom.
This book is theirs in more ways than I can count.

CHAPTER ONE

INTRODUCTION

Most of the people of the world live and die without ever achieving membership in a community larger than the family or tribe. Except in Europe and America, the concerting of behavior in political associations and corporate organizations is a rare and recent thing.

Edward C. Banfield, *The Moral Basis of a Backward Society*

This book concerns the familiar phenomenon known as schooling. It departs from the usual approaches to education in that the problems of instruction and its direct outcomes are of peripheral interest. The main argument rests on the observation that schools and the classrooms within them have a particular pattern of organizational properties, different from those of other agencies in which socialization takes place, and on the contention that what children learn derives from the nature of their experiences in the school setting.

The image of schools and schooling is shaped by familiar observations. American public schools are part of both the municipal and state polities, staffed by adults, and concerned with the instruction of children between the ages of, roughly, five and twenty. They are known by their division into distinctive levels (elementary, junior high, and senior high), by their departmentalization according to subject matter, and by the character of their administrative hierarchies. Instruction and, one hopes, learning take place primarily in classrooms and consist mainly of situations in which the teacher imparts, and the students acquire, symbolic skills, information, and national tradition. Although this brief listing scarcely exhausts the important characteristics of schools, familiar observations soon leave off and less obvious ones begin.

First, schools are found in industrial societies or in the industrialized sectors of societies which are otherwise nonindustrial. All societies provide arrangements for raising children and for their development into adults; that is, "education" is universal. However, only in certain societies do children obtain their education by leaving a unit of kinship to enter a markedly different social organization not controlled by kinsmen. Herskovits, for example, contends:

A much more restricted sense of the word 'education' limits its use to those processes of teaching and learning carried on at specific times, in particular places outside the home, for definite periods, by persons especially prepared or trained for the task. This assigns to education the meaning of schooling.[1]

Second, although schooling takes place in a setting both geographically separate and socially distinct from his family of orientation, the child continues his membership in and close contact with his family.[2] At the conclusion of schooling, the child—more correctly, the young adult—leaves the family of orientation, establishes a family of procreation, and becomes employed in an occupation. In industrial societies these last three events represent the main defining characteristics of adult status.[3] Schooling, therefore, should be viewed as a transitional phase linking stages in the life cycle.

Third, the school constitutes a component of a larger network of social institutions that includes the family, adolescent peer groups, occupations, and other institutions organized around the expression of the political, religious, and leisure activities of adults. That is, it represents a link not only between successive phases of the life cycle but between the private realm of the family and the larger public domain.

The school, then, is an organizational embodiment of a major social institution whose prime function is to bring about developmental changes in individuals. It is an agency of socialization whose task is to effect psychological changes that enable persons to make transitions among other institutions; that is, to develop capacities necessary for appropriate conduct in social settings that make different kinds of demands on them and pose different kinds of opportunities. Inkeles has stated:

Socialization research generally begins from the wrong end. . . . The starting point of every socialization study should be a set of qualities 'required' by, i.e., maximally adaptive in, a given socio-cultural system and/or manifested in a given population. The task of students of socialization should be to explain how these qualities came to be manifested by individuals, thus rendering them competent, or why individuals failed to manifest these same qualities, thus being rendered less competent to perform in the given social setting.[4]

This work is a theoretical exercise designed to explore the properties of an agency of socialization and its place within a larger network of institutions. It begins with the assumption that individuals, by acting in a situation, cope with the constraints of that situation and use the opportunities it provides. The nature of these constraints and opportunities varies with the properties of the situation. For example, if there are rules prescribing conduct in one setting and not in another, individuals in the first setting must work out ways of coming to terms with the rules; they may obey them all the time, obey them under some circumstances but not under others, subvert them, or evade them. In the second setting, the problem of coping with the rules does not arise. Similarly, small and enduring groups afford individuals few opportunities for the free selection of acquaintances; large groups, in contrast, open up these opportunities, but it remains for the individuals to decide how to make use of them. In small groups, they must cope not with the problems that free choice presents but with the problems presented by closed alternatives. Over time, individuals learn how to cope with and adapt to situations of various kinds. Depending on their successes and failures, they learn, implicitly or explicitly, what works and what doesn't, and the principles underlying these alternatives.

Before children enter school, most of their time is spent in the family, where they have learned how to get along with parents, siblings, more distant relatives, and neighbors. There are many ways to get along in family settings, but all of them are oriented to the conditions characteristic of family life and the problems posed by it. When children enter school, presumably they can apply to the new setting some of the patterns of conduct already learned at home; for example, responsiveness to the requests of adults, respect for the desires of other children, and the like. But the school presents new demands not previously confronted at home, and children must learn new ways and new principles of conduct for dealing with them.

It is well known, of course, that not all families are alike; some have many children, some have few; some have children widely spaced in age, while the children in others are narrowly spaced; some have a parent absent, others are intact; parents may be more or less affectionate, arbitrary, punitive, indulgent. Thus, depending on actual family circumstances, there will be variations in the ways children cope with the family situation and in the principles of conduct they learn to consider appropriate. Similarly, schools differ. Some are large, others are small; some are graded, others are ungraded; some employ ability grouping, others do not; and certainly teachers vary in their styles of instruction and discipline.

Although I acknowledge these familiar variations in both family and school, it is not my intent to make this an empirical study in which variations in one set of conditions are related to variations in another; therefore it is not possible to take into account the differences known to exist. Instead, the strategy is to consider modal patterns, common elements believed to exist despite known variations. There are inevitable distortions in this kind of procedure, but the choice to adopt it rests on the assumption that the main trend will be captured even though, in a different kind of investigation, one would have to take these distortions into account. Moreover, I believe, the formulation presented here can be translated into terms subject to empirical investigation.

The substance of the argument, then, goes as follows: If schooling forms the linkage between the family life of children and the public life of adults, it must provide experiences conducive to learning the principles of conduct and patterns of behavior appropriate to adulthood. I am concerned here only with the experiences that schooling provides for the transition between family life and later participation in the polity and in the occupational sector of the economy.[5] Although schooling undoubtedly contributes to the acquisition of knowledge and skills through instruction, these developmental changes constitute only components of the total outcome. I am concerned, however, not with these traditional symbolic outcomes, but with what I believe to be normative outcomes that emerge through pupils' experiences in coping with the sequence of situations whose character is defined by the structural properties of schools. These outcomes, then, are formulated not in terms of the explicit goals of the schools, but in terms of the schools' peculiar relevance to family life and to the occupational and political worlds.

The state of psychological knowledge has not yet developed to the point where it is possible to indicate just how children learn what they do from their experiences in a variety of social settings. Much more is known about the learning of discrete skills and the solution of discrete problems in experimental settings than is known about the learning of relatively enduring behavior patterns, moral principles, and styles of response over time and in less clearly defined naturalistic settings such as families, play groups, schools, and the like. Accordingly, speculation and the fragmentary findings of isolated research efforts are all that is available to fill the gaps in our knowledge about the critical questions of inducements, motivations, and symbolic media that make it possible for children to learn principles of conduct by inference from their social experiences. Any adequate answer to the question of what is learned in school must await a massive empirical effort based on a clear formulation of the elements of school and classroom organization, of the instructional process, of the relevant motivations and inducements, and of the outcomes of schooling.

NOTES AND REFERENCES

1.   Melville J. Herskovits, *Man and His Works*, p. 310, Alfred A. Knopf, New York (1949). Wilson, in a paper concerned with teachers, states that ". . . teachers exist as a specialist profession only in advanced societies. In static societies values, techniques, and skills and what are taken to be 'facts' are transmitted from father to son. If specialist activities are developed at all, their skills and the mystique which accompanies them is [sic] learned from practitioners not from teachers, and the learners are apprentices

rather than pupils." Bryan R. Wilson, "The Teacher's Role—A Sociological Analysis," *British Journal of Sociology* **13**, No. 1, 15 (1962). Both Wilson and Herskovits imply that the existence of a distinct teaching occupation is characteristic of societies in which schools are distinct organizational entities. It should be added, though, that if teaching is an occupation, a society that has teachers must have an occupational system, and such societies are industrial. Herskovits goes on to distinguish schooling from enculturation, which refers to assimilation of elements of culture with and without direction from others. He distinguishes both from education although he defines the latter only by example; it is unclear whether education includes the other two or whether it is a distinct process in its own right. He then goes on: "The significance of the distinction between 'schooling' and 'education' is to be grasped when it is pointed out that while every people must train their young, the cultures in which any substantial part of this training is carried on outside the household are few indeed. When we treat of education, we must again consider the important place specialization plays in machine cultures, as against its relative absence in nonliterate societies." Herskovits, *ibid.*, p. 311. Whether specialization is the crucial factor here must remain moot.

2. One exception to this generalization is the case of boarding schools; pupils attending them do not actually relinquish their membership in the family of orientation but rather have less contact with its members.

3. There are obvious exceptions to and variations in this generalization. Graduation from school may be followed by college or military service and the postponement of marriage and employment. Some people do not marry, few are never employed; there is no one prescribed sequence among these events, though in the absence of special circumstances, employment does not usually follow marriage by too long a time.

4. Alex Inkeles, "Social Structure and the Socialization of Competence," *Harvard Educational Review* **36**, No. 3, 282 (1966).

5. I do not deal with other institutional areas, such as those organized around the activities of adolescent peer groups, religious organizations, leisure and recreational pursuits, and the like despite their acknowledged importance and relevance to the schools.

CHAPTER TWO

THE SOCIAL STRUCTURE OF FAMILY AND SCHOOL SETTINGS

The extremely close connection between the age of pupils and the organic structure which gathers them together gives each year a personality of its own: the child has the same age as his class, and each classroom and its master a distinctive complexion.

Philippe Aries, *Centuries of Childhood*

We know from personal experience, if we recall our schooldays, the importance which a difference of a few years had in our childhood and youth. We know how we set our schoolmates' ages against the average of our class, which was our only standard of comparison; our understanding of childhood or youth or adolescence depended on an academic hierarchy, first a succession of classes, then the passage from secondary to higher education.

Philippe Aries, *Centuries of Childhood*

There is little question but that schools are engaged in an instructional enterprise, but the nature of the school experience is a question of broader dimension. It concerns the structural characteristics of schools as well, because children's experiences are no less tied up with them than they are with curriculum and the activities of instruction. The familiarity of the school's characteristics obscures their nature; they snap into focus, however, when the school is compared with some other setting such as the family. Consider, for example, the phenomenon of yearly promotion, a fact that appears almost too trivial to mention. There is nothing analogous to it in family life despite clear resemblances in the functions of the two settings and their strong influences on the lives of children during the same phases of the life cycle. The implications of the presence and absence of this characteristic, then, command attention.

I turn to the identification of the school's structural properties through comparison with those of the family. This is an appropriate comparison because it links two agencies that are involved in a developmental process and are related both sequentially and contemporaneously. I shall compare these two social settings in terms of the following dimensions of structure: (1) boundaries and size of social settings, (2) duration of social relationships, (3) relative numbers of adults and nonadults, (4) composition of nonadult characteristics, (5) composition of adult characteristics, and (6) visibility among nonadults.

STRUCTURAL CHARACTERISTICS OF SCHOOLS AND FAMILIES

1. Boundaries and Size of Social Settings

Families are unitary in their social organization in the sense that they lack formally defined subdivisions. School systems are divided into levels and, within each level, into classroom units in which most of the instructional activities take place. Considering the main activities of both families and schools, the kinship unit composed of parents and dependent children and the classroom composed of teacher and pupils are directly analogous. The number of individuals comprising the membership of classrooms is almost always larger than that of families, the latter being numerically small units rarely having as many as 10 members, whereas classes rarely contain that few. Secondary school classrooms are slightly smaller, on the average, than those of primary schools,[1] although there are substantial local variations in this relationship which are attributable in part to changes in rates of birth and migration.

TABLE 1.   The Relationship between School Level
           and Mean Size (Enrollment)

Level	Mean Size	No.
Elementary	705.7	189
Junior High	1194.9	150
Senior High	1773.6	162

According to information collected as part of the National Principalship Study, the mean enrollment of schools at each level, at least in large cities, varies as shown in Table 1.[2] School size, on the average, is larger at each more advanced level.

For the purposes of this inquiry, the importance of school size lies in its implications for composition, because larger schools serve larger areas. Public schools serve distinct geographical districts whose population varies not only in size but in composition. Since families tend to reside among others having similar social characteristics, and since they differ in income, religion, ethnicity, and other characteristics related to residential location, the larger the district, the greater its social heterogeneity. Because they serve the residents of larger districts, secondary schools are, on the average, more heterogeneous in pupil composition than elementary schools.

2.   Duration of Social Relationships

Until a child is old enough to attend school, he spends the greater part of each day among members of his family, mostly with his mother and pre-school siblings, but also with neighbors. At the start of school, the child, now a pupil, usually spends a substantial portion of each day away from his family and in the company of a teacher and other children, people not related to him by kinship, in a classroom. He returns to his family at the close of each school day. During the elementary years, he spends most of every schoolday with one or a small number of teachers.[3] At the end of each school year his association with the teacher ends, and at the beginning of the next year, he has a new teacher. His relationships with family members, however, continue unbroken even though the amount of contact with them is less than during the preschool years, and decreases somewhat through the remainder of his elementary schooling as he develops interests that take him away from home.

In secondary school, and more so in high school than in junior high, pupils divide their time among several teachers each day (roughly an hour a day with each instructor of a major subject), and spend less time with any one teacher than in elementary school. Each of these relationships ends at the conclusion of the year. In addition, more time is spent away from home, much of it taken up with activities with peers, often without adult participation or supervision.

In summary: though children leave the family to attend school, they continue their active membership and participation in it. The device of annual promotion from grade to grade affords them a type of experience in school that is unavailable to them in the family, that of serially establishing and severing relationships with adults. Usually a child does not terminate close and intense relationships with members of his family until late adolescence, and even then those relationships only become more attenuated and less demanding in time; they are not severed, like the relationship with last year's teacher. As a child proceeds through elementary to secondary school, the pattern of forming and breaking relationships increases in frequency because he faces a larger number of teachers at that level than at the former.

3.   Relative Numbers of Adults and Nonadults

The importance of both absolute and relative numbers in social life has been described by several observers. Nisbet, for example, has shown that verbal development in children is inversely related to family size,[4] and Simmel, most notably in his classic treatment of two-person groups, three-person groups, and minorities, has worked out the psychological and political implications of number for the establishment of trustfulness, secrecy, and the formation of coalitions.[5] Although there are many ways to formulate the concept of "number," I shall use it here to indicate opportunities for social conduct among members of the two social settings: families and classrooms.[6]

The number of persons occupying the constituent positions of families and schools affects their distinctive character as settings in which teaching and learning take place. To adequately describe the settings, however, we must make several assumptions. First, the units being compared are the family and the classroom, and for present purposes, both are somewhat problematic. In American society, the conjugal family is the appropriate unit of kinship, one in which the conjugal bond between husband and wife is of prime importance, but not to the exclusion of relationships between nuclear members of the family and more extended kin. For convenience, however, and with only a minimum of distortion, this discussion will be based on the nuclear family, a unit consisting only of a conjugal pair and dependent children.[7] The classroom is the predominant instructional unit in the school, and although both larger and smaller units (for example, large lecture audiences and small homogeneous groups distinguished according to members' abilities) are used for certain instructional purposes, none has yet replaced the classroom with its isolated teacher and aggregate of pupils.

Second, in each setting there is a formal distinction between adults and nonadults: parents and children in the family, teachers and pupils in the school, with the adult members in each having distinct advantages in power and in control over sanctions and resources.

Third, there is a characteristic pattern in the timing of school events. Schooling is cyclical in that nearly all instructional events take place during each five-day school week; that is, with the exception of special events, one week is like another (the content of subject matter changes, of course) in a way that one day is not necessarily like another. The passage of time will be treated here *as if* the distribution of events occurring over a week could be applied to each day. Even though family life is not periodic in the same way, I shall assume in both school and family that time is homogeneous over the short-run, that the distribution of events of one day is reasonably similar to that of the next.

Fourth, even though sex differences and sex ratios of parents and children, teachers and pupils, may be important for what is taught and learned in each setting, these differences will not be explicitly taken into account here.

Fifth, there are several social conditions that may affect the number of pupils in classrooms, independently of school level, the most obvious being the size of the school system[8] and differing rates of birth and migration. Throughout the discussion, I shall assume that these conditions and their associated effects, if any, remain constant.

TABLE 2. Ratios of Adults and Nonadults in Two-Parent Families

Children per family	Children/Adult	Adults/Child
One	0.50	2.00
Two	1.00	1.00
Four	2.00	0.50
Six	3.00	0.33

There are no more than two parents in a family, but there may be one or more children.[9] American families are small social units, at least in comparison to classrooms, and to the extent that two parents and their dependent children are present, likely increases in the number of children will not change the relative numbers of children and adults sufficiently to produce large shifts in the ratios between them, as illustrated in Table 2.

In classrooms there is typically one adult member, the teacher. The number of adult members does not differ much from the number of parents in the family, but the number of pupils differs markedly from the number of children in a family. According to figures collected by the National Education Association, elementary teachers have a mean class membership of 29.1 pupils, and secondary teachers have a mean class membership of 26.6 pupils.[10] That is, there is very little difference between levels in the average number of pupils who assemble for each class meeting.

This statement does not necessarily apply to the average number of *different* children who appear in a given teacher's classroom each day. In elementary schools in which any one teacher[11] has the main responsibility for instructing the same children all week, roughly 29 different pupils receive instruction from each teacher. In secondary schools, organized on a departmental basis, in which a teacher[12] faces a procession of pupils in a sequence of class meetings each day of the week, an average of 155.8 *different* pupils receive instruction from each teacher. The sharp discontinuities between family and classroom settings appear in the ratios of nonadults to adults:

Six-child families	3:1
Elementary classrooms	30:1
Secondary classrooms	160:1

Although families and classrooms resemble each other in that both contain adult and nonadult positions, the disparity in ratios (notice that including the six-child family diminishes the disparity between home and school) indicates the vastly different opportunities these settings provide for expressing personal interest and for making claims on time and energy. Clearly, the chances afforded children to establish relationships of dependency with teachers similar to those they maintain with parents are small; likewise, teachers are unable to devote attention and show personal consideration to each child the way parents can. Moreover, the numerical properties of classrooms reduce the possibility that teachers can establish and maintain authority through the formation of close emotional ties with individual pupils. Instead, when the occasion arises, the teacher must employ means designed to exercise authority over the members of the classroom collectively as well as over individuals within it.

4. Composition of Nonadult Characteristics: Homogeneity–Heterogeneity

In comparing families and schools, one finds differences in the distribution of personal attributes of nonadults in each setting. Dependent children in nuclear families are alike in social status, by definition, and in ethnicity, race, and religion (save in some cases of adoption). They differ in age and sex, and in their various abilities and physical attributes.

The distribution of these characteristics in elementary classrooms contrasts with their distribution in families. Since elementary schools draw pupils from residential neighborhoods, the composition of classrooms resembles that of the neighborhoods in social class, ethnicity, race, and religion. Although elementary classrooms are more heterogeneous in composition than nuclear families, they are less so than secondary classrooms whose pupils come from much larger residential districts. The sex composition of both families and schools is mixed, random in the former and roughly equal in the latter; in any case, there is no prescribed or preferential distribution except in noncoeducational schools.

Of all these attributes, age is the most exceptional. We tend to keep maturational time by the clock of age in whatever time units are appropriate (e.g., weeks and months with infants, years with older children and adolescents). Within limits it is expected that, during specified age spans, children will possess certain physiological and psychological attributes, capacities, and skills, and will engage in certain activities. The children born to one set of parents almost always differ in age (with the obvious exceptions of one-child and multiple-birth families), but whereas families cannot eliminate age differences among children, schools can and do by admitting a like-aged group to the first grade and carrying it through for twelve years. In recent years, some elementary schools have experimented with nongraded arrangements in which clusters of grades, containing a two- or three-year age spread but rarely more than that, are treated as a unit. Nongrading, of course, constitutes an exception to the strict definition of age homogeneity. This is not a disqualifying exception, however, because the age span is not that much broader and the phenomenon is not that widespread. The phenomenon is exceedingly rare at the secondary level, so that after several years of elementary schooling, pupils encounter an extended period of narrowly homogeneous age grouping.

Differences in the ages of children in families with two or more can range from under two years to (rarely) as many as twenty. Despite their smaller membership, the age-spread within families is likely to be larger on the average than that within classrooms. Unlike the previously-mentioned characteristics of nonadults (in which classrooms are more heterogeneous than families), classrooms are more homogeneous with respect to age.

Age differences among children in a family lie at the root of many of the most controversial issues in domestic life, issues that are compounded when sex differences are also considered. In content, many events and activities in which age or sex differences are important, such as table manners, bed-time, ownership of toys, are ostensibly trivial, while others, such as privileges, responsibilities, suitable rewards and punishments, supervision, appear more weighty. In either case, children's interests are at stake in that questions of fairness and equity with strong emotional overtones are usually involved. Boys and girls may be very close in age, but boys often receive less parental supervision. Older children are expected to accept certain onerous obligations from which younger siblings are exempt; they may also be more severely punished than younger children for the same misdeeds because they are supposed to "know better." In such circumstances, reminding them of the compensating privileges that accrue because of their age does not always convince them of how well-off they are.

Describing the age and sex differences of children is one thing; describing the family as a social setting in terms of these characteristics is something else. For this discussion, the most important fact is that families are social units in which one rarely finds two persons alike in age *and* of the same sex. These two characteristics in combination are almost invariably sufficient to identify each family member, and they constitute prime reference points for conduct in many spheres of social life.

Schools, in which classrooms are the most important social units, contrast sharply with the family. Elementary school classrooms tend to be homogeneous in composition, though less so than families. Even though schools at this level tend to serve fairly circumscribed residential districts, the homogeneity is far from complete; it is, however, far greater than that of secondary schools. The main difference between elementary classrooms and families is age composition, based on the biological facts of birth order on one hand, and, on the other, statute law, which usually requires that school attendance begin at age six.[13] In time, the age range in a given grade expands somewhat, but this expansion is slight, especially since the advent of automatic promotion. The matching of age and grade is always problematic; there are difficulties when children of like abilities but widely differing ages are found in the same grade, and when a grade is made up of children of about the same age who differ widely in ability. Witness the present trend toward nongraded instruction and the older devices of "skipping" and "leaving back" as organizational provisions for coping with these two problems.

Throughout all the years of schooling, pupils sitting in any given classroom resemble each other in a great many ways. This statement, however, conceals about as much as it illuminates, especially those differences between secondary and elementary schools that so prominently appear when attention is shifted from classrooms to schools. Although pupils attend school with their equals in age, by the time they enter high school, they have been formally differentiated into tracks or curricula, largely, though not completely, on the basis of prior academic achievement. The tracks are organizational properties of secondary schools (high schools, actually) and are distinguished in terms of difficulty and content. The main distinction among tracks is between the college preparatory and the others leading ultimately to occupations not requiring a college education. Pupils assigned to each track attend classes with others having roughly comparable academic records and capacities, although there is considerable variation in the performance of pupils within the same track. Each track is designed so that pupils receive instruction which will qualify them for various jobs. Even though preparation for future *employment* (emphasized in the more vocationally oriented tracks) is an important consideration governing the form and content of the secondary curriculum, the schools should not be thought of as narrowly vocational in either purpose or function.

TABLE 3. The Membership Composition of Families and of Elementary and Secondary School Classrooms*

| | | CLASSROOMS | |
	Family	*Elementary*	*Secondary*
Social Class	1	2	3
Religion	1	2	3
Ethnicity	1	2	3
Race	1	2	3
Sex†	i	d	d
Age	3	1	1

* On a continuum of homogeneity–heterogeneity: 1 = homogeneous, 2 = intermediate, 3 = heterogeneous

† Sex composition is either divided (= d), roughly equal numbers of males and females; or indeterminate (= i).

Elementary schools differ from secondary schools in that elementary pupils resemble each other in their social characteristics in much the same way that families in the neighborhood do. This same generalization holds within classrooms, except that in addition there are often informal and somewhat fluid groupings formed on the basis of capacity and/or achievement. These elementary school ability-groupings differ from the secondary school tracks in their fluidity and in their absence of formal recognition. Pupils with different histories of academic performance who have differentiated themselves to a point where they cover a broad range

THE SOCIAL STRUCTURE OF FAMILY AND SCHOOL SETTINGS

of academic performance are re-equalized, or re-homogenized, on entering high school. Thus, in secondary schools with a track system, pupils who differ markedly in the quality of their academic work do not customarily receive instruction in the same classroom. In schematic form, the situational properties of families, elementary schools, and secondary schools, based on the composition of personal and social characteristics of the members, are shown in Table 3.

5. Composition of Adult Characteristics: Homogeneity–Heterogeneity

The concept of "parent" refers to *one* social position within every family and is defined on the basis of generation. Differences between parents in social characteristics and in their modes of conduct related to sex are of basic importance in raising children. As far as adult membership is concerned, families always differ in sex composition; the social class, ethnic, racial, and religious composition of parents is usually homogeneous for each characteristic.[14] Although there are customary preferences about age, there are variations in the relative ages of parents.

The main criterion for determining the composition of a teaching staff is subject-matter competence, with standards usually based on training and experience. Other teacher characteristics are taken into account explicitly or implicitly, and the most obvious of these is sex. Schools at the three levels differ in the sex composition of their faculties, but elementary schools are overwhelmingly staffed by females. In elementary schools, as Herriott and St. John indicate, there tends to be a rough correspondence in the composition of both pupil groups and teacher groups according to race and religion.[15] Teachers are expected to be competent in activities that differ with the level of school in which they work. In elementary schools, with the exception of certain specialized subjects that occupy only a small segment of the pupils' school week, each teacher holds responsibility for instructing pupils in all or most areas of the curriculum. This generalized competence forms the basis of the so-called self-contained classroom of the elementary school, a type of classroom organization that has given way to some extent to quasi-departmentalized arrangements such as team teaching.

In secondary schools, the situation differs in that teachers are expected to have command of one major subject-matter area (perhaps as many as two or three[16]) and to have mastered a relatively narrow segment of the total curriculum and the techniques for teaching it. In addition, there is formal provision for the so-called guidance services (including, among other things, remedial work, college placement, vocational planning, psychiatric referral, modified forms of psychotherapy, psychological testing, and personality assessment), designed to deal with a variety of psychological problems that arise during the course of schooling. With the exceptions of college and vocational planning, these same tasks are performed in elementary schools, even though at this level there is usually no formal, permanent division of the school staffed by guidance specialists. Much of this work is done by teachers and by specialists who serve elementary schools on a visiting basis or through consultation.

To summarize: In composition, the adult membership of nuclear families is sexually heterogeneous (if the term heterogeneous can be used to describe a two-member group), and usually homogeneous in terms of age. Even though there tends to be a sexual division of labor between parents in the raising of children,[17] there is considerable overlap in child-rearing activities, and parents have latitude in determining what that division shall be. However, they are not trained specialists in the raising of children.

In elementary schools, each teacher is expected to have mastered several instructional skills and areas of knowledge, to be a generalist of sorts. An elementary school staff tends to be relatively homogeneous in its composition, if mastery of instructional skills is taken as the prime consideration, in that all teachers have a similar broad repertoire of skills and substantive knowledge (with variations according to the grade taught).

At the secondary levels, and more in senior than in junior high schools, the teaching staff tends to be heterogeneous, with each teacher responsible for a specialized subject area or areas. Organizationally, secondary schools are departmentalized by subject matter within the instructional area and between the instructional and guidance areas. Neither families nor elementary schools are departmentalized.

6. Visibility among Nonadults

Both families and schools afford their nonadult members opportunities to see each other in a variety of situations and over different spans of time, to observe others, learn about them, and judge them.[18] In families, there are many occasions for children to observe each other; they live together in the same household for many years, especially when they are close in age, and see each other in a variety of different situations: with and without adults, with and without other children, at work and at play, engaged in a variety of activities, in different moods, and when, as observers, their presence is known and unknown. Family members, then, have chances to see a lot of each other, and, as they get older, to think about what they observe.

The opportunities for pupils to observe many facets of the lives of other pupils at school are more circumscribed than in the family, because there are more people to observe and because school attendance tends to be more transient. In addition, the variety of observable situations and activities is more limited. More specifically, a great deal of what pupils see of each other is linked in many ways to the instructional activities directed by the teacher. Thus, even though classrooms afford ample opportunities for observation, the range of events and activities taking place is narrower than in the family.

A classroom has certain characteristics of a public place, more so than does a family. Many activities are carried on out loud and in front of everybody: reports, recitations, replies to questions, discussions, praise, chastisement, instruction, laughter. Activities are frequently initiated by the teacher, and pupils are required to engage in public performance, often judged openly by the teacher and by other members of the class. Formal marking, both for assigned work and for general evaluations of performance over a period of several months, is customarily done in some degree of privacy. Once pupils receive marks, however, whatever confidentiality is maintained by the teacher in their assignment tends to be short-lived, since pupils themselves turn private into public knowledge.

It would be incorrect to claim that the quality of performance, academic and otherwise, is of no interest to children in the same family; however, the family provides opportunities for children to see many additional facets of each other's lives that the school does not and cannot provide for classmates. At the same time, family life—it would be more correct to include other aspects of nonschool life as well—affords children greater opportunity for unobserved, unjudged privacy (housing conditions permitting). Schools, and more specifically classrooms, are designed for a much narrower range of activities than families. Whatever the special character of these activities (the topic of a later section), the classroom is organized in such a way that they can be easily and constantly observed.

EXPERIENCES RELATED TO FAMILY AND SCHOOL CHARACTERISTICS

Several implications emerge from the foregoing comparison of the structural properties of families and schools. The traditional notion of learning as a function of teaching, of engagement in instructional activities, may be an overly restricted view of what happens during the schooling process. There is no reason to doubt the importance of both the content and methods of instruction; acknowledging its importance, however, is not the same as identifying those learning outcomes for which it is important and those for which it is not, although it is widely recognized that little is known about the effects of various teaching methods and styles of classroom management on learning outcomes.[19] The fact is that both families and schools, two settings in which children seem to show marked psychological and behavioral changes, have structural properties that may affect learning in characteristic ways through the different experiences they provide for children.

First, schooling would appear to bring about *additions* to the psychological repertoire, not to undo or replace in any fundamental sense the products of prior learning in the family. This contention appears warranted from the fact that children continue their active and participatory membership in the family while they proceed through the successive phases of schooling. That the impact of schooling appears to be one of accretion rather than displacement is consistent with the fact that individuals remain members of some family unit during their whole lives, and must always know how to act in ways to sustain appropriate relationships among kinsmen. Some settings, in contrast to schools, are designed to regulate social life so that the quality of relationships among kin is rendered inappropriate. Seminaries for the training of a celibate clergy are a case in point. Others, such as army relocation centers and officer candidate schools, are designed to change people's ways of conduct and thinking away from patterns no longer appropriate to previous social circumstances. In cases of this kind, membership in the prior setting is terminated before efforts to bring about change have begun.[20] If continuing membership in the family promotes learning patterns of conduct appropriate to units of kinship and similar settings, then schooling, I contend, contributes to learning patterns of conduct appropriate to that and related settings. The first walk from home to school, then, symbolizes the beginning of an extended process in which children learn to adjust their conduct to the different settings in which they find themselves.

Second, schooling demands the formation of social relationships more transient, more time-bounded than those characteristic of the family. The small size of the family, the great frequency of contact among its members and particularly between mothers and children, the intensity of emotional bonds, and the mutuality of support make it a setting well suited for establishing relationships of dependency. The school provides a much larger pool of individuals within which a pupil establishes relationships. Annual promotion, moreover, limits the duration of these relationships to about one year, and ensures, at least with those formed with adults, that they will be broken. The school, then, constitutes a setting more conducive than the family to the formation of looser, more fluid social bonds inconsistent both with strong ties of dependency, and with authority based on enduring personal obligations to elders.

Third, school provides for the formation of more diverse relationships than are found in the family; it affords pupils opportunities for contact with children from a greater variety of backgrounds than life at home and in the neighborhood provides, and this more at the secondary levels than at the elementary.

Fourth, schooling provides experiences for learning the distinction between social positions and the persons who occupy them. Both families and classrooms are two-position settings, each with its own particular division into adult and nonadult. The distinctive characteristic of classrooms is that the membership of the adult position is systematically varied, since, unlike parents, teachers are attached to grade levels and not to a particular group of children whose school career they follow all the way through. A pupil receives instruction from different individuals every year, each of whom fills the position of teacher. This arrangement makes it possible to establish the independence of persons and positions they occupy.

Fifth, the arrangement and operation of classrooms provide experiences in which evident differences among pupils are subordinated to similarities in their characteristics and situation. In the family, individual differences, particularly age during childhood and both age and sex during adolescence, form the basis for relatively unique treatment even though all children are members of a single family unit. In the classroom, by contrast, differences in social status, ethnicity, race, religion, sex, and physical attributes reflect the composition of these relatively visible characteristics in the school district; yet within the classroom, all pupils very close in age and in capacities related to age, occupy a single position, are given similar work assignments, confront the same teacher, and are treated very much alike in instructional and disciplinary matters. Stated differently, under these conditions, much more than in the family, pupils have an opportunity to view each other and themselves as sharing common experiences, and as being in the same boat despite the obvious personal differences among them.

Sixth, the public and collective nature of the classroom, the visibility of its members to each other, and the parity among them, provide opportunities for each as part of an overwhelming majority to observe and judge the actions of other members individually and at the same time observe the judging process in which the teacher and the other members participate, a situation well-constructed for the public sanctioning of individual persons.[21]

Seventh, the high school track system functions to re-equalize members of the same age group who have differentiated themselves academically during previous years of schooling. Traditionally, the track system is seen in terms of its distributive function of steering individuals toward one or another broad segment of the occupational hierarchy, and in terms of its allocative function for the larger society by which occupational positions become filled by persons possessing appropriate capacities.[22]

The continuing preoccupation with the allocative and distributive functions, emphasizing the school's linkage with its external environment, has contributed to the neglect of other questions, in particular, the internal implications of the track system for learning in classrooms. The effect of tracking within the school is to make classroom composition more homogeneous in terms of pupil ability than it would be if pupils were assigned to classes randomly or on the basis of some criterion unrelated to achievement. A teacher with a heterogeneous class in which a wide range of academic abilities are represented finds himself with good reason to treat pupils as special cases[23] and to adjust his instructional activities accordingly. Similar adjustments are not as necessary in homogeneous classrooms. It is much safer to treat all pupils as if they were alike when there is some assurance that a given set of tasks will not be unreasonably demanding to some and hopelessly unchallenging to others.

In describing some of the structural properties of families and schools, I have attempted to delineate the nature of the experiences that are available to children in these two settings and that play such a crucial part in their psychological development. The picture has been deliberately drawn with broad strokes, and, like all attempts to portray the main outlines of a scene, it obscures and distorts some familiar realities. Not all families are intact, not all children come from nurturant homes, not all elementary schools are more homogeneous in composition than high schools, not all young children attend school in neighborhood districts, and to the extent that conditions described earlier in the chapter do not obtain, the experiences believed to derive from these conditions are not likely to materialize. Yet, I would maintain, the picture represents the mode, the dominant pattern, the differences between school and family that occur more frequently than not.

To say that experiences related to structural arrangements are available is to put the argument conservatively; simply on the basis of a structural analysis, it is premature to conclude that each child actually *has* the experiences. Yet it would not be farfetched to assume that many and probably most do have them. Available experiences, even if the opportunities afforded by them are taken, are not the same as learning outcomes; they represent an intermediate step based on the assumption that the experiences must be present if people are to learn from them. But whatever may be the importance of the structural properties of families and schools in shaping the experiences of children, the behavior of children and adults participating in each setting will be equally important. Accordingly, I turn in the next chapter to the description of dominant patterns of conduct, again in modal terms, characteristic of family and school settings.

NOTES AND REFERENCES

1. According to the NEA, the mean size of classes taught in elementary schools is 29.1; in secondary schools (junior and senior high combined) it is 26.6. *National Education Association, The American Public School Teacher,* (1960–61), Research Monograph 1963-M2, pp. 50, 52 (1963). The Coleman Report provides a consistent but slightly different picture. For elementary schools, the average number of pupils per instruction room is 30; per teacher it is 29; for secondary schools, the corresponding figures are 31 and 23. U.S. Department of Health, Education, and Welfare, *Equality of Educational Opportunity,* pp. 67, 69, U.S. Government Printing Office, Washington (1966).

2. Robert Dreeben and Neal Gross, "The Role Behavior of School Principals," p. VI-37, U.S. Office of Education Final Report No. 3, (August 1965). The sample used in this study included 501 nonteaching school principals, representing 5% of the 10,956 principalships in 41 American cities of population 50,000 and over in 1960. It was stratified according to region, per-pupil expenditure, city population, school level, and the socio-economic level of the school district. *Ibid.,* p. III-3. Note that these figures apply only to urban schools.

3. There are variations in this pattern insofar as children spend time with various educational specialists in addition to one or a few teachers; in team teaching situations, children have contact with more teachers in the course of a day than in the more traditional, self-contained elementary school classroom.

4. John Nisbet, "Family Environment and Intelligence," in A. H. Halsey, Jean Floud, and C. Arnold Anderson (eds.), *Education, Economy, and Society,* pp. 273–287, Free Press of Glencoe, New York, (1961).

5. Georg Simmel, *Sociology,* translated by Kurt H. Wolff, pp. 107–110, 118–175, Free Press, Glencoe, Ill. (1950).

6.   For a similar usage, see Seymour Martin Lipset, Martin A. Trow, and James S. Coleman, *Union Democracy,* pp. 154–175, Free Press, Glencoe, Ill. (1956). See especially pp. 162–163, dealing with the opportunity for the voluntary formation of friendships and its bearing on political participation.

7.   The concepts of conjugal and nuclear family are similar and can be used interchangeably when one is talking about particular family units rather than about the kinship system characteristic of a society. For a good discussion of the distinction, see William J. Goode, *The Family,* pp. 51–52, © 1964. Reprinted by permission of Prentice-Hall, Inc., Englewood Cliffs, N.J. "All contemporary studies in the most industrialized societies—Great Britian and the U.S.—show that in fact each family unit maintains contact with a wide range of relatives, . . . [and] that many of these relatives *outside* the conjugal unit cannot be cut off without annoying or hurting someone *inside* the family." *Ibid.,* p. 51. The effect of using the nuclear rather than the conjugal family as the unit is to omit consideration of a few additional adults and children, omissions that would have very little effect on the ratios to be discussed.

8.   In a study of public school teachers, the NEA noted that in systems employing one to 49 teachers, the mean number of pupils per classroom was 24.9; in systems with 2500 or more teachers, the mean was 32.3. There were consistent step-wise increases in the mean corresponding to increases in system size. *The American Public School Teacher,* p. 51.

9.   In 1964, of families in the United States with one or more related children under age 18, 80.6% had from one to three children; of the families with one or more own children under age 18, 80.7% had from one to three. U.S. Bureau of the Census, *Statistical Abstract of the United States: 1965* (86th edition). Table 38, p. 37, U.S. Government Printing Office, Washington, D.C. (1965).

10.   *The American Public School Teacher,* p. 50. Note that the study distinguishes between elementary and secondary teachers, not schools.

11.   A "classroom teacher, teaching all or nearly all subjects to *one* class." *The American Public School Teacher,* p. 102.

12.   A "classroom teacher, teaching a specific subject or subjects to several different classes." *The American Public School Teacher,* p. 102.

13. The law does not pertain solely to attendance, but usually defines in addition what "six-year old" means. Children over and under that age are not eligible for first grade. Eligibility regulations are easily seen as solutions to potentially nagging administrative problems, but in effect they also limit school enrollment in the earliest grades to a very narrow age group.

14. Intermarriage by religion, race, or ethnicity is an exception to this statement.

15. Robert E. Herriott and Nancy H. St. John, *Social Class and the Urban School,* pp. 76–83, John Wiley and Sons, New York (1966).

16. I do not refer here to those situations in which teachers are compelled to offer instruction in courses for which they have had little or no preparation because no teacher qualified in the subject is available.

17. See, for example, Morris Zelditch, Jr., "Role Differentiation in the Nuclear Family: A Comparative Study," in Talcott Parsons and Robert F. Bales, *Family, Socialization, and Interaction Process,* pp. 307–342, Free Press, Glencoe, Ill. (1955); Fred L. Strodtbeck, "Family Interaction, Values, and Achievement," in David C. McClelland *et al., Talent and Society,* pp. 135–191, Van Nostrand, Princeton (1958); Bernard C. Rosen and Roy D'Andrade, "The Psychosocial Origins of Achievement Motivation," *Sociometry* **22,** No. 3, 185–218 (1959).

18. For a general discussion of visibility see Robert K. Merton, "Continuities in the Theory of Reference Groups and Social Structure," in *Social Theory and Social Structure,* (revised edition), pp. 319–322, 336–340, Free Press, Glencoe, Ill. (1957).

19. For a rigorous critique of the literature in the area, with particular emphasis on problems of measurement and research design, see Robert E. Herriott, "The Influence of Teacher Behavior upon Changes in Pupil Behavior: An Appraisal of Empirical Research," unpublished manuscript, Cambridge, Mass.; Harvard Graduate School of Education, 1960.

20. For a discussion of army relocation centers, see Robert K. Merton and Alice S. Kitt, "Contributions to the Theory of Reference Group Behavior," in Robert K. Merton and Paul F. Lazarsfeld (eds.), *Studies in the Scope and Method of 'The American Soldier,'* pp. 95–99, Free Press, Glencoe, Ill. (1950). Brainwashing represents another type of situation that demands the severance of previous social ties; see Edgar H. Schein, "The Chinese Indoctrination Program for Prisoners of War," *Psychiatry* **19**, No. 2, 149–172 (1956). Military academies represent still another type of setting where a break, although not as sharp a one, is required; see Sanford M. Dornbusch, "The Military Academy as an Assimilating Institution," *Social Forces* **33**, No. 4, 316–321 (1955).

21. For a poignant but over-interpreted description of collective sanctioning, see Jules Henry, *Culture Against Man*, pp. 295–302, and *passim*, Random House, New York (1963).

22. The allocative aspect of the track system has been discussed as a theoretical question by Talcott Parsons, "The School Class as a Social System: Some of its Functions in American Society," *Harvard Educational Review* **29**, No. 4, 297–318, and especially 313–317 (1959); and as an empirical question in Seymour Martin Lipset and Reinhard Bendix, *Social Mobility in Industrial Society*, pp. 227–259, University of California Press, Berkeley (1951); Joseph A. Kahl, *The American Class Structure*, pp. 276–298, Rinehart, New York (1957); and Richard M. Stephenson, "Mobility Orientation and Stratification of 1000 Ninth Graders," *American Sociological Review* **22**, No. 2, 204–212 (1957).

The distribution question also has its ideological side; whether members of the economically disadvantaged sectors of society have access in proportion to their numbers to the more rewarding positions in society if they have the capacities to meet the demands imposed by these positions. See for example, W. Lloyd Warner, Robert J. Havighurst, and Martin B. Loeb, *Who Shall Be Educated*, Harper and Brothers, New York (1944); and J. E. Floud, A. H. Halsey, and F. M. Martin, *Social Class and Educational Opportunity*, William Heinemann Ltd., London (1956).

23. For a more general discussion of the problem of special cases in organizations where groups of persons are treated both individually and similarly, see Alfred S. Stanton and Morris S. Schwartz, *The Mental Hospital*, pp. 301–341, Basic Books, New York (1954).

CHAPTER THREE

PATTERNS OF CONDUCT IN FAMILIES AND SCHOOLS

One's failure is paraded before the class minute upon minute, until, when the worst spellers are the only ones left, the conspicuousness of the failures has been enormously increased.

Jules Henry, *Culture Against Man*

The typical investigation of the impact of teacher behavior on learning outcomes deals with methods of instruction and styles of classroom management, often formulated in ideological terms, and with indications that the explicit goals of the school, measured as individual psychological products, have been achieved. In this discussion I am concerned not with these questions but with patterns of activities designed to elicit desirable conduct on the part of children. They represent some of the central tasks of families and schools, and without them neither setting would be recognizable as such. Earlier, I dealt with those parts of children's experience shaped by the structural properties of schools and families; here, I consider aspects of their experiences shaped by their own conduct and that of teachers and parents.

Sociologists often interpret patterns of behavior by attributing them to prevailing norms, to evaluative standards that define how individuals should act in various situations. When a norm can be identified and individuals shown to act according to it, we speak of conformity (as, for example, when motorists follow traffic signals, or patients follow a doctor's orders). Events of this kind, however, cannot be understood solely in terms of conformity to and deviation from norms; there are other considerations involved: sanctions, questions of legitimacy, the characteristics of persons involved, the substance of issues between the individuals, ecological arrangements, and so on.[1]

Norms and behavior are analytically independent, their empirical relationship problematic. Thus (1) norms may be acknowledged and widely accepted, yet people will deviate from them; motorists pass red lights even though traffic signals are about as unequivocal as normative "statements" can be. (2) Some norms explicitly allow for variations in conduct; for example, there are variable standards for how actively people should participate in political campaigns. When norms vary, just what types of behavior represent conformity, deviance, or variance are difficult to determine. (3) Certain patterns of behavior are not understandable simply as conforming or deviating responses to normative standards. For example, there are predictable circumstances under which people will temporize, not because they conform to a norm to temporize or because they deviate from a norm to act promptly, but because they are caught up in a situation offering no acceptable alternative for acting. Thus, any adequate formulation relating norms to behavior must take into account at least these three different phenomena.

This discussion will proceed on the assumption that norms and behavior are related, that individuals act in a given situation as if they were conforming to the prevailing norms, even though under the circumstances this may not be the case. My purpose in adopting the assumption is to describe, *in modal terms,* certain norms and behavior characteristic of family and school life as they pertain to the experiences in which learning takes place.

EXPRESSING AFFECTION

The expression of affection among family members is prescribed conduct, but this is not to say that all members of a family act affectionately to one another. As one observer put it: *"Members of the conjugal family are obligated to help one another because they are* kin *and love one another.''*[2] Expressions of affection, both physical and verbal, take many forms; support, nurturance, sympathy, and acceptance all represent the bases on which solidarity is established among family members.

Bonds of affection are expected to endure over time even though events occur in which affectionate responses are not appropriate. Hostility and matter-of-factness are acceptable modes of family behavior, clearly appropriate to many situations but not predominant in the behavior of kinsmen over the long run. In other words, unlike parties to a commercial transaction, family members do not customarily deal with each other at arm's length or with hostility, unless a specific situation calls for it. Moreover, since the family is a small group, and since its members spend much time together, the opportunities for expressing affection are great.

Although affection is not proscribed in schools, it is expressed less intensely and under more limited circumstances. In the long run, matter-of-factness in the accomplishment of specific tasks governs the relationship between teachers and pupils, and teachers are customarily expected to be friendly but to avoid intense expressions of either verbal or physical affection.

As noted earlier, schools differ from families in that the number of pupils in a classroom far exceeds the number of children born of two parents; in addition, a secondary school teacher faces more pupils per day than his elementary school counterpart. Schools also differ in having formal provision for severing the relationship between teachers and pupils established over an academic year. On both counts, classrooms are settings in which teachers are expected to avoid establishing enduring relationships with pupils premised on affection. To paraphrase an earlier statement, both the adult and nonadult members of a classroom are expected to help and like one another because they are engaged in performing a multitude of individual and collective tasks, and not because they love one another.

THE ACTIVITIES OF ADULTS AND NONADULTS

In both families and schools, all members have jobs to do that are appropriate to the setting. In the family, there is a division of labor in which certain tasks are allocated to men and women, adults and children. Other tasks, many in number, are performed by any member or combination of members without categorical identification as to sex, age, or generation. The basis of assignment can be complex. There are certain household chores, like shoveling snow, that are not performed by very young children, that are performed by older children regardless of sex, and that are performed by older boys (more than girls) and adults.

Even though labor is divided in the family, many of its component activities, particularly the most important ones concerned with the raising of children, cannot be readily described in terms of a job description because they do not have a clear beginning, end, or time duration; because one act or sequence of acts may represent the performance of several different tasks at the same time; and because there are many permissible ways of doing the same thing. Perhaps most important, the goals of family life are expressed only in the most general way and not specified in terms of the performance of discrete, contributory acts. If raising children to have certain desirable characteristics is one of these goals, the qualities and capacities that parents hope to create almost defy precise definition, and the means available to them do not have any precise articulation with the goals however defined.

Yet parents continue to raise their children according to their ideas about when and how to show affection, punish, advise, question, assign responsibility, supervise, encourage, blame, and so on through the whole repertoire of activities, operating on the assumption that the activities they engage in at given times and in particular situations express their intentions,[3] and that those activities lead to the achievement of whatever goal, immediate or long-term, they have in mind.

The idea of "goal," or "purpose," leaves much to be desired when applied to family life, particularly in the raising of children. In general terms, one purpose is to get children to grow up, to become adults, and in American society this means leaving the family of orientation, getting married, and getting a job. *"In a sense, [parents] are partially occupied with forcing the child to develop so that he can leave the family."* [4] The parental activities involved in this process are too numerous to catalogue here, but include instructing children about the physical, personal, and social realities of their environment and how to cope with them, sanctioning their behavior, and expressing a broad range of beliefs, judgments, and emotions about events both within the family and outside it.

Events occurring in classrooms are narrower in scope than events occurring in the family, although both settings resemble each other in the indeterminacy of the relationship between their respective means and ends. In school, however, teachers explicitly and systematically ascertain the outcome of instructional activities even if they cannot always establish the connection between the outcome and the activities designed to produce it. It is more reasonable to speak of the goals of classroom instruction (mastery of symbolic skills, acquisition of information, learning manual skills, and so on) than of family child-rearing because relatively tangible indications of them can be obtained. For example, it is possible to administer tests that measure competence in reading or the acquisition of factual material without knowing for sure whether the results can be attributed to the contribution of the school or to agencies outside of it.

Despite evident similarities, most classroom activities differ from those of the family. The central core of them is instructional in that teachers assign the pupils specific tasks to perform and then assess the quality of their performance. In the early elementary school years these tasks consist of basic cognitive skills necessary for pupils to learn reading, writing, and the manipulation of numbers. These same skills can be learned from family members, and often are, yet it is school time rather than time at home that is devoted primarily to their acquisition. Teachers assign the same or similar tasks to all pupils in a classroom, with some modifications based on levels of ability, and evaluate performance by formal testing. Despite the fact that parents are far from indifferent to how well their children perform both at home and in school, family life does not customarily involve this form of evaluation, in which the performance of one child is compared systematically with that of others on the same task and over the same period of time. In fact, evaluation of this kind would be very difficult in the family because children differ widely in age-related capacities.

It would be erroneous to claim that task performance and its evaluation, however important, are all that occurs within classrooms. There are provisions for other activities as well, including games and schoolwide events, and occasions for informal social contacts both among pupils and between pupils and teachers. More at the elementary than at the secondary levels, teaching combines friendliness, nurturance, and affection with the task-oriented engagement of pupils in instructional activities and their evaluation. (As described earlier, certain noninstructional components of secondary schooling tend to be included among the functions of specialized guidance departments.)

The differences in activities comprising family and school life are extremely important. In the family, there is no normative or empirical priority between performance of day-to-day activities and emotional expression; both must occur if the members are to sustain themselves physically and remain together in solidarity. However important the social and emotional considerations for motivating pupils and encouraging them to participate in the school regime, the school's *explicit* purpose and *official* reason for existence lie in the area of instruction: imparting the skills, information, and beliefs each child will eventually need as an adult member of society. However necessary the expressive aspects of schooling are to the accomplishment of its performance goals, the latter justify the former, and not the other way around; beyond the prevailing standards of everyday decency and friendliness, emotional expressiveness serves the instructional goals of schooling.

In summary, the school is an organization primarily concerned with the encouragement of activities in which children demonstrate how well they can achieve; its adult members assign specific tasks to its nonadult members who in turn are expected to perform them and submit the results for evaluation. In so doing, pupils distinguish themselves from each other over a period of years on the basis of their achievement; and although teachers are likely to consider the quality of performance in the various cognitive activities most seriously (in recognition of their later occupational importance), that quality does not represent the sole criterion by which pupils are differentiated.[5]

SANCTIONING

In both family and school, certain patterns of action are encouraged and discouraged by rewards and punishments which take the form of both specific acts and more enduring patterns of action.

I assume that when enduring patterns of behavior are encouraged and discouraged, a sustained relationship between the persons involved must exist, one that involves more than the reward and punishment of specific acts on a *quid pro quo* basis. Whatever else its weakness, an arrangement based on exchange would require those involved to maintain such surveillance of each other that each desirable act received its reward and each undesirable one its punishment. As Durkheim and others have indicated, patterns of social life cannot continue if the contractual terms of each action must be settled each time.[6] In the family, the basis for encouraging and discouraging children's behavior lies in their dependence on parents from earliest infancy and the mutual expression of love and affection; a relationship, in other words, analogous to good will in the economic sense. Although rewards for specific actions can replenish this bank of good will, the existence of the bank is not itself a reward nor is it filled only by rewarded acts. Rather, it is maintained by gratuitous support, friendliness, interest, sympathy, encouragement, and the like, not as responses to specific acts, but as indications of a more enduring solidarity. Punishment, then, even if severe, means one thing if administered in the context of a sustained relationship of affection and another where such feeling is absent.

Problems of reward and punishment confront teachers as well as parents. At the start of their schooling, the experiences children have had with rewards and punishment have been limited primarily to the family. Since classrooms are structured differently than families, as are the activities of the adults and nonadults in each setting, the problems of reward and punishment also tend to differ.

First, since children in classrooms outnumber those in families, teachers, for reasons of limited time and energy, cannot sanction each child as much or in the same manner that his parents can; a teacher must be able to control a class without sacrificing the school agenda to the imperatives of keeping some semblance of order. Moreover, a teacher does not have at his disposal those emotional resources for the exercise of authority that are characteristic of the family; resources based on intimate association in a very small group and on a prolonged relationship of warmth, nurturance, acceptance, withdrawal of affection, and even physical punishment. Second, pupils' academic performance is customarily sanctioned by means of the grades teachers assign according to the quality of specific units of work. There is nothing inherently rewarding or punishing in the letters, numbers, and words conventionally assigned as grades. Prior to their first encounter with school, children's behavior is not judged primarily on a specific task for specific sanction basis (and, if it is, only to a limited extent), and parents do not usually reward and punish their children with grades or other discrete symbolic forms of recognition. One central problem of early elementary schooling, then, is for teachers to establish grades *as* sanctions, that is, to get pupils to regard high grades as rewarding, low grades as punishing. To the extent that pupils do not learn to accept them as such, grades cannot serve the function of rewarding good performance and punishing poor. Secondary schools, and to some lesser extent the later years of elementary schools, operate according to the assumption— not always correct—that pupils have already come to accept the sanctioning quality of grades.

The problem confronting elementary school teachers, then, resembles that of parents with young children; to treat them so that they come to regard certain symbolic and physical expressions as rewards and punishments. As a prerequisite, the parents' initial job is to develop a relationship of love and nurturance with their children; analogously, the elementary school teacher's first job is to create among pupils a diffuse and positive attachment both to herself and to the school.

THE STRUCTURAL BASIS OF SCHOOL SANCTIONS

In the first grade, a formal and prolonged process of separating children from the family begins. It does not involve severing or renouncing kinship ties nor does it require relinquishing the normative principles of family life, since most members of society remain part of some kinship unit throughout most of their lives. School does, however, put demands on pupils to give up, in certain situations, principles and patterns of behavior they have come to accept as family members; more precisely, it requires them to restrict the premises governing family life to conduct among kinsmen, and to adopt others—new, strange, and even painful—that apply to settings outside the family. At the outset, schooling may provide but few of the gratifications of family life, and then only in attenuated form, until pupils discover sources of gratification in schooling itself, an outcome by no means universal or inevitable.

It should not be assumed that schooling is by nature an alien experience nor one for which young children are entirely un- prepared. They differ in their interest in and capacities for doing school work; some have learned the rudiments of the basic cognitive skills and have had experience in school-like social situations before entering the first grade. Many parents provide their children with opportunities to act independently, stress the importance of achievement and competence, and create a home environment in which reading, talking, and thinking have a prominent place. Yet even with prior preparation, school represents a considerable departure in a child's existence.

Little is known about how elementary teachers create gratifications for their pupils out of resources available in the school. They cannot assume that grades will be automatically rewarding, although undoubtedly some children have already learned to value grades before starting school. Also, by rigorously enforcing standards of self-reliance and achievement in the earliest grades and by expecting pupils to accept responsibilities incommensurate with their capacities, teachers may create undue pressure and discouragement for the pupils. Although a pupil can gain a sense of competence and gratification from his successes, extracting gratification from public failure poses a problem in psychological alchemy. Parents make allowances for their young children and help them with tasks beyond their existing capacities, but teachers, because of their responsibility for a class of like-aged pupils both as a collectivity and as an aggregate of individuals, are unable to give each one the special attention he may have grown accustomed to at home.

Aside from the fact that they lack the resources for sanctioning available to parents and cannot necessarily rely on the effectiveness of grades, teachers must confront certain technological weaknesses in their position. Little is known, for example, about how to persuade individuals gathered in a public place to be cooperative, how to diagnose one's own errors in the near absence of qualified observers or reasonably reliable methods of assessment, or how to create the desire among pupils to bring collective pressure on each other to advance the instructional enterprise.[7] In terms of power, the teacher's position is vulnerable. Ostensibly positive sanctions are often found problematic; not all pupils are drawn to the lure of grades, and nonacademic incentives may pale in comparison to the intrinsic pleasures of making life difficult for teachers. Ostensibly negative sanctions often bring diminishing returns; punishments meted out too often lose their punishing quality, and pupils who have survived the worst a teacher can dish out cease to be awed by what might be in store for them next time. In effect, the teacher, consciously or not, must rely to a considerable extent on personal resources for gaining the necessary respect and affection from the large number of pupils who assemble daily in classrooms.

The substance of sanctioning problems differs according to school level. At the elementary level, teachers must use their available resources so that pupils come to like school, accept the prevailing rules of the game, find gratification in doing school work, and learn to accept as rewarding the symbolic expressions that teachers intend them to experience as rewarding. At the secondary level, problems arise when teachers incorrectly assume that the elementary school has done its job; thus pupils will experience the sanctioning qualities of grades only if they have learned to acknowledge them as such during the elementary years.

Teaching involves a classic problem in the creation of goodwill; finding in the classroom some equivalent to affection and support in the family, those forms of gratuitous pleasure not tied to *specific* acts in a relationship of exchange. There is a distinction, for example, between a teacher smiling when a pupil has done a particular task well and smiling as a characteristic demeanor with no direct connection to any specific (approved of) act. A form of expression such as the latter is not negotiated act-by-act (a smile for ten words spelled correctly), and, although it is not negotiable in this sense, a general relationship of friendliness between teacher and pupils may nevertheless affect the terms of exchange even if it is not such a term itself.[8] What the components of goodwill are (e.g., whether the teacher likes the pupils, smiles, talks kindly, acts encouragingly, etc.), remains a matter of conjecture. Conditions for the creation of goodwill, however, probably include associations between persons that endure beyond each social transaction as well as the successful use of *generalized* resources such as the expression of positive emotion.[9]

There are several structural characteristics of classrooms, all discussed earlier, that when considered in combination, identify the resources available to teachers for sanctioning. I am concerned not with such rewards and punishments as grades, compliments, criticisms, and the like exchanged for specific manifestations of discrete skills and conduct, but with more generalized sanctions providing resources for the acquisition of norms. A classroom is a public place in that membership is collective and visible. Its nonadult members are alike in one crucial respect, their age. Age is crucial because it represents an index (even if inexact) of developmental maturity, and, by implication, of capacity.[10] (Pupils are roughly alike in other characteristics besides age, particularly in certain social attributes related to neighborhood residence.) Homogeneous age composition is important in two senses: (1) It provides classrooms with a built-in standard for comparison, a fixed point indicative of those pupil capacities directly relevant to the activities in which they are engaged. Each pupil, then, can be compared and can compare himself with all others because the comparisons can be anchored to the standard. (2) It allows each pupil the experience of finding himself in the same boat with others in terms of the characteristics of their social surroundings and in the way they are treated by teachers.

Since many classroom activities are judged in public, the pupil is bombarded with messages telling him how well he has done and (with a short inferential leap) how good he is. If he doesn't take the teacher's word for it, he need only look at the performance of others of the same age and in the same circumstances. The school, in effect, plays on his self-respect. Each pupil is exposed and vulnerable to the judgments of adults in authority and of his equals, those who resemble him in many respects.[11] If the child at home wonders whether he is loved, the pupil wonders whether he is a worthwhile person. In both settings he can find some kind of answer by observing how others treat him.

Given the standards for and patterns of behavior that children learn from their family experiences, the schools, in preparing them for adult public life, must effect changes of considerable magnitude, changes that require giving up certain patterns of conduct found gratifying in other settings and adopting new patterns whose gratifications may at best take the form of promissory notes. If knowledge about other forms of socialization is applicable to schooling, and there is no reason in principle why it should not be, the sanctions required must affect people's emotions deeply, as is true in some of the most demanding and stress-creating social situations involving psychological change: psychotherapy, religious conversion, brainwashing, deracination. It is my contention that the emotions aroused in schooling derive from events in which the pupil's sense of self-respect is either supported or threatened, and that school classrooms, permitting the public exposure and judgment of performance against a reasonably fixed reference point (age-adapted tasks), are organized so that the pupil's sense of personal adequacy, or self-respect, becomes the leverage for sanctioning. The effectiveness of the leverage, of course, is not determined by its availability, and many conditions will determine pupils' susceptibility to it.

Not all sanctions employed in school settings have the potentiality for arousing intense emotions, nor are they similarly diffuse in character. Some are contingent: grades, compliments, admonitions, chastisements in exchange for desirable and undesirable conduct; others are noncontingent: friendly greetings, gentleness, sympathy, sarcasm, bitchiness, and so on through the whole gamut of words, gestures, and postures indicating approval and disapproval. All represent resources at the teacher's disposal, used consciously or unconsciously, which influence the pupils in deciding whether or not they will find their early experiences at school enjoyable enough to act according to the standards governing school activities.

NOTES AND REFERENCES

1. Attempts to identify the various psychological and sociological elements linking norms and behavior and the relationships among these elements are generally classified under the heading of role analysis. For recent conceptual contributions to this area of inquiry, see Neal Gross, Ward S. Mason, and Alexander W. McEachern, *Explorations in Role Analysis,* pp. 48–69, John Wiley and Sons, New York (1958); and Daniel J. Levinson, "Role, Personality, and Social Structure in the Organizational Setting," *Journal of Abnormal and Social Psychology* **58,** No. 2, 170–180 (1959).

2. William J. Goode, *World Revolution and Family Patterns,* p. 24, Free Press of Glencoe, New York (1963). ". . . the small marital unit is the main place where the emotional input-output balance of the individual husband and wife is maintained, where their psychic wounds can be salved or healed. At least there is no other place where they can go. Thus, the emotions within this unit are likely to be intense. . . ." Goode, *ibid.,* p. 9.

3. For example, parents who watch over their children much of the time may do so to express how much they care about the children's welfare, but at the same time and by the same means may communicate a sense of distrust.

4. William J. Goode, *The Family*, p. 78, © 1964. Reprinted by permission of Prentice-Hall, Inc., Englewood Cliffs, N.J.

5. Parsons, for example, distinguishes between cognitive learning: ". . . information, skills, and frames of reference associated with empirical knowledge and technological mastery"; and moral learning: ". . . 'deportment' . . . responsible citizenship in the school community. Such things as respect for the teacher, consideration and co-operativeness in relation to fellow-pupils, and good 'work-habits' are the fundamentals, leading on to capacity for 'leadership' and 'initiative,' " Talcott Parsons, "The School Class as a Social System: Some of its Functions in American Society," *Harvard Educational Review* **29,** No. 4, 303–304 (1959).

6. Emile Durkheim, *The Division of Labor in Society,* translated by George Simpson, pp. 200–229, Free Press, Glencoe, Ill. (1949).

7. "Collective approval of power legitimates that power. People who consider that the advantages they gain from a superior's exercise of power outweigh the hardships that compliance with his demands imposes on them tend to communicate to each other their approval of the ruler and their feelings of obligation to him." Peter M. Blau, *Exchange and Power in Social Life,* p. 23, John Wiley and Sons, New York (1964).

8. Parsons treats this issue by distinguishing ". . . the *contingency* of what alter (the agent of care) does on what ego (the child) has done or is expected to do, . . ." from ". . . the component of *generalization*. There exist not merely discrete, disconnected sanctions, but a pattern of relatively systematic and organized sanctions. . . ." Talcott Parsons, "Social Structure and the Development of Personality: Freud's Contribution to the Integration of Psychology and Sociology," in *Social Structure and Personality,* p. 87, Free Press of Glencoe, New York (1964).

9. Parsons, for example, commenting on Freud's contribution to understanding personality development, states: "[Childhood eroticism] can be regarded as, essentially, a built-in physiological mechanism of the *generalization* of internal reward. . . . Erotic pleasure seems to be essentially a diffuse, generalized 'feeling' of organic well-being which is not attached to any one discrete, instinctual need-fulfillment." Talcott Parsons, "Social Structure and the Development of Personality: . . ." p. 90.

10. Perhaps the social expectations for and beliefs about the capacities of similar-aged children are narrower than their actual capacities (however these are measured). If so, age is an exaggeratedly "good" index of equal capacity even if the goodness is a self-fulfilling prophesy.

11. " 'Remember that you are as good as any man—and also that you are no better.' . . . [But] the man who is as good as his neighbors is in a tough spot when he confronts all of his neighbors combined." Louis Hartz, *The Liberal Tradition in America*, p. 56, Harcourt, Brace, New York (1955). The coerciveness of massed equals is not negligible.

CHAPTER FOUR

NORMATIVE OUTCOMES OF SCHOOLING

The distinctive competence [of an organization] to do a kind *of thing is in question.*

Philip Selznick, *Leadership in Administration*

Traditional approaches to understanding the educational process have been concerned primarily with the explicit goals of schools as expressed in curriculum content: the cognitive skills involved in reading, arithmetic, and the like; subject matter content, national tradition; how to think; vocational skills; and a multitude of good things such as citizenship, self-confidence, tolerance, patriotism, cooperation, and benevolent attitudes of various kinds. They have also been concerned with pedagogy: methods of instruction considered broadly enough to include motivation and quasi-therapeutic activities as well as didaction more narrowly conceived. One indication that curriculum and pedagogy occupy a central place in educational thinking is the existence of a massive literature reporting research devoted overwhelmingly to problems in these two areas and to evaluations of instructional effectiveness in bringing about curricular outcomes.[1]

There is no question but that schools are engaged in an instructional enterprise, and by the same token, so are families. Parents instruct their children in ways similar to those of teachers and in similar areas of cognitive development.[2] Many children learn to read, count, and do simple arithmetic before they ever arrive at school, and parents complement and supplement the teachings offered by the school as well as provide instruction in areas outside its standard curriculum. Although strains arise in family life when parents involve themselves in the instruction of their children, strains attributable in part to the incompatibilities of engaging in task activities in the same setting in which affectional ties are of great importance,[3] they also arise in classroom settings. As their children's schooling proceeds, parents become less and less adept as instructors. This is primarily because some of the subject matter becomes too specialized, not because families are inappropriately structured for carrying on instructional activities. On a society-wide basis, family instruction may be unstandardized and lacking in scope, but this faults the family as an agency of instruction primarily on grounds of inefficiency, not incompetence.

Both instruction and knowledge, even at high levels of sophistication and specialization, are readily available outside both the school and the household through the mass media, travel, museums, libraries, and personal contacts with a great variety of people. Perhaps the greatest teacher of them all is the street.[4] Clearly, the school has no monopoly as an instructional agent, and unless one is willing to accept the rather implausible notion that two major social institutions—the family and the school—can be so strikingly different in structural properties and still serve highly similar functions for the rest of society, the school's peculiar competence must lie elsewhere.

Certain of the school's organizational characteristics, such as the division of high schools into subject matter departments and into tracks, are usually understood in terms of their relevance to instruction. Although departmentalization is clearly related to curriculum content, the fact that many persons, each responsible for different subjects, all occupy the single position of teacher means that this organizational arrangement is related to the cluster of experiences in which pupils learn the distinction between persons and positions. Similarly with the track system: tracks are distinguished according to post-high school destination, with the curriculum of each, despite overlap, related to that destination. There is no necessary reason, however, why recruitment to college and to immediate post-high school employment cannot be tied to the cumulative achievement records of pupils who have spent their high school years in heterogeneous classrooms rather than in the relatively more homogeneous ones comprising the various tracks. Again, the arrangement appears to contribute to an outcome of schooling not directly tied to instructional objectives.

Although the dissemination of knowledge and teaching of skills are certainly part of the school's agenda, the evidence for its characteristic set of structural properties and for the fact that other agencies serve similar instructional functions suggests that what is learned in school is not restricted to what is taught nor, more strongly, restricted to that which is *teachable pedagogically*.

To the question of what is learned in school, only a hypothetical answer can be given at this point, one that considers outcomes related to the experiences of pupils and tied to their participation in a social setting whose characteristics I have identified: *pupils learn to accept principles of conduct, or social norms, and to act according to them*. Implicit in this contention are the following assumptions: (1) Tasks, constraints, and opportunities available within social settings vary with the structural properties of those settings; (2) individuals who participate in those tasks, constraints, and opportunities derive principles of conduct (norms) based on their experiences in coping with them; and (3) the content of the principles varies with the setting. Most importantly, the acceptance of social norms represents but one outcome of schooling; it is not the sole one.

Norms are situationally specific standards for behavior; they are principles, premises, or expectations indicating how individuals in specifiable circumstances *ought* to act. For example, pupils are expected to arrive at school on time. To say that they accept this norm means that: (1) there is such a standard whose existence can be determined independently of the pupils' behavior (in this case, the distribution of times they actually arrive at school); and (2) pupils adhere to the standard in the sense that they consider that their actions should be governed by it. Acceptance, then, refers to a self-imposed, acknowledgeable obligation of variable intensity. The content of the norm must be in somebody's mind and communicable by gesture, spoken word, written rule, or sanction.[5]

There are both logical and empirical problems in using the concept of "norm." First, norms and behavior must be distinguished analytically because it is logically circular to infer norms from behavior and then use them to account for variations in behavior. Second, norms must be distinguished analytically from values, although this is easier said than done. Values also refer to preferences but are not specified as to situation or conduct.[6]

Third, although norm acceptance and behavior are analytically distinct, the relationship between them must still be formulated logically. The acceptance of norms is a variable, and refers to the extent to which a person imposes obligations on himself, to how intensely he holds them. Difficulties of measurement aside, the degree of acceptance can vary between internalization, holding a deep inner conviction whose violation induces anxiety or guilt, and cynical agreement. Whatever the extent of norm acceptance, there is a range of possible behavioral responses; for example, actions vary in frequency relative to a given norm and according to prevailing conditions. Since there is variation both in the degree of norm acceptance and in the relationship between the norm and the behavior oriented to it, behavior cannot be viewed simply as a matter of conformity to or deviation from norms.

Fourth, a variety of conditions can affect the relationship between norm acceptance and behavior. (1) People may disagree about what norm applies in a particular situation; behavior in situations where consensus is lacking may not represent conformity to any of the conflicting norms. I refer here to situations of role conflict or cross-pressures such that people are caught in situations in which they must choose between the lesser of two evils, or in which a desirable outcome is accompanied by undesirable consequences. People often cope with such situations by withdrawing, compromising, temporizing, and the like; their behavior must be interpreted as coping with the demands of a situation characterized by normative conflict and not simply as conformity or deviance.[7] (2) Behavioral conformity may depend on the explicitly or implicitly conditional nature of norms. For example, although lying is proscribed in principle, there are widely acknowledged situations in which telling white lies is acceptable.[8] (3) There are variations in people's desire to conform; they calculate the likelihood and severity of punishment if they do not conform; judge the opportunities, ecological and otherwise, to conform or deviate; and determine what their interests are.

The ostensibly straightforward contention that the peculiar contribution of schooling is that pupils learn social norms should not conceal the problematic nature of that concept (schooling) and the complex relationship between norm acceptance and behavior.[9] More specifically, schooling helps pupils to learn what the norms are, to accept those norms, and to act according to them. Norm content, acceptance, and behavior can all vary independently. Goode, for example, reminds us: "... *internal [emotional] commitments [to an adequate discharge of ... role duties] are not sufficient to maintain even a single role relationship. Ample commentary, both literary and historical, exists to show that under certain types of situations men will abandon even well-learned role responsibilities: ...*"[10] In other words, if there is indeterminacy in the relationship between norm commitment and behavior, it is likely that there is also indeterminacy in the relationships among norm content, acceptance, and behavior, although indeterminacy does not imply randomness in these relationships.

The concept of social norm has long been important in sociological thinking where it has been considered primarily as a determinant, a prior condition to account for some pattern of behavior, whether as an external constraint, rule, expectation, and sanction, or as an internal force, obligation, conviction, and internalized standard. If a pattern or rate of behavior is observed, a characteristic procedure of sociological interpretation is to ask, among other things, whether it represents conformity to or deviation from a norm, or whether it is a phenomenon that emerges from a situation in which norms "operate." There has been comparatively less attention paid to the question of how norms originate in social settings and how individuals learn them.

To argue that normative outcomes emerge from the process of schooling in the absence of clear and substantial empirical documentation requires some demonstration that the contention is plausible and defensible. Certainly, there is no evidence to the contrary; just as certainly, there is evidence supporting some of the key linkages that would have to be established in order to document the proposition appropriately: (1) that the acceptance of norms can be effected through programmatic efforts, (2) that the experiences of members of an organization can be related to variations in organizational structure, (3) that changes in norms or other psychological states can be made without reliance on didaction, and (4) that there is some symbolic vehicle that can mediate the learning of principles of conduct.

One recent venture in understanding the creation of norms originates in experimental and personality psychology; namely, McClelland's training program for the acquisition of achievement motivation.[11] His vocabulary comes from psychology, not from the sociological study of norms. Despite the differences in words, the program for developing achievement motivation includes the tasks of informing subjects about what achievement is, getting them to impose on themselves the obligation to achieve, and encouraging them to act according to this obligation; that is, to learn the content[12] of a norm, accept it, and act in conformity to it. According to McClelland, *". . . motives are affectively toned associative networks arranged in a hierarchy of strength or importance within a given individual."*[13] Sociologists do not use this language to talk about norms (witness the earlier statements of Blake and Davis, and Goode), but the procedures McClelland employs to arouse achievement motivations, derived from his definition, suggest that accepted or self-imposed norms and motives are virtually the same thing as far as the individual is concerned.

With respect to content, for example, his subjects perform tasks designed to instruct them in the meaning of achievement motivation: *". . . we teach them how to code and how to write stories saturated with n Achievement; in fact, that is one of the basic purposes of the course: to teach them to think constantly in n Achievement terms."* [14] Another phase of the program, concerned with norm acceptance, is designed *". . . to give the subjects a set or a carefully worked-out associative network with appropriate words and labels to describe all its various aspects . . . The power of words on controlling behavior has been well documented."* [15] The key word here is "controlling," to guide one's own actions according to a particular scheme of ideas. The sense of acceptance, or obligation, has at least two sources in the program: first, thinking about a large variety of situations in achievement terms; and second, assessing one's current level of achievement and finding it unsatisfactory. *". . . we point out that if they think their score is too low, that can be easily remedied. . . .*[16] *The next step in the course is to tie thought to action. Research has shown that individuals high in n Achievement tend to act in certain ways."* [17]

The program for developing the need to achieve is designed to create both the associations and the emotional involvements called for in the definition of motive. The conceptual scheme implicit in the definition, however, contains no explicit provision for defining the characteristics of the social arrangements in which the program was offered. From evidence drawn from a fragmentary description, the program lasted a few weeks in a residential setting and was carried out in classroom-like settings, using various teaching devices, as part of voluntary management training institutes. The structure of the setting, it appears, was not considered to be a problematic question. There is reason to believe, though, that the nature of settings is a matter of some importance. It is noteworthy, moreover, that in other settings designed to bring about personality change, such as mental hospitals, colleges, professional schools, religious seminaries, and the like, residential or other arrangements are commonly employed to assure separation from customary social pressures and associations, and both frequent and intense contact among participants.[18]

STRUCTURAL VARIATIONS
IN SOCIALIZATION SETTINGS

In a discussion of the structural properties of socialization settings, Wheeler considers ". . . *the attributes of these organizations that are likely to lead to different socialization outcomes for persons who pass through them. The focus is on the organizational context of socialization and on the way in which differently organized settings may produce different socialization experiences.*" [19] He develops a typology based on two cross-cutting dimensions: (1) the social context of recruits, whether they enter as individuals or as members of collectivities, and (2) the social composition of other members, whether recruits have been preceded by others in the same position (serial), or whether there have been no predecessors (disjunctive).[20]

Wheeler's paper considers three main organizational issues: goals, the passage of clients through the organization, and its relationship to the external environment. Subsumed under each is a discussion of apposite structural properties, such as: characteristic rates of interaction, role differentiation, social climate, and modes of entry and exit, to name but a few. In general, Wheeler compares two or more organizations on some dimension or dimensions and points to the implications of the compared characteristics for the socialization experience of clients. In connection with

NORMATIVE OUTCOMES OF SCHOOLING

membership composition, for example, he observes that public schools have a clientele similar in age (by grade) and marital status and different in sex and socio-economic status. Prisons, in contrast, have a membership whose composition is opposite on these four dimensions. By implication, he contends:

Youthful inmates of 20 may be exposed to what may be either a steadying or a depressing influence on their immediate adjustment *and* future aspirations. *Faced with 70-year-old men who have lived most of their lives in institutions, or with married men who are worried about their wives' fidelity or who are receiving divorce papers, they may encounter reasons for developing* a fatalistic attitude *toward the future, quite apart from whatever component of a criminal value system they find around them.*[21]

Wheeler's main interests in his paper explicitly exclude a systematic formulation of the psychological outcomes of socialization settings, although the emphasized phrases in the preceding paragraph indicate his awareness of the problem. (McClelland, in contrast, deals with one specific psychological trait.) There is no attempt, for example, to determine whether attitude and aspiration are similar psychological phenomena or whether a given setting is more likely to be hospitable to the formation of one kind of outcome than another. By and large, the outcomes are broad in their definition; adjustment, as in the previous paragraph, *"change in skill level, . . . reconstruction of . . . personality,"* and others throughout the text. These limitations belong to the field in its undeveloped state rather than to Wheeler's paper, and to identify them is to add to the agenda for further investigation. The paper, however, provides clear justification for treating the structural properties of organization as problematic in terms of the acquisition of social norms.

NORMATIVE CHANGE WITHOUT DIDACTION

In a highly original study of socialization, Breer and Locke have investigated the impact of social experience on the formation of ideas, treating both situation and outcome as problematic. In a general summary of their work, they state:

It is our thesis that in working on a task an individual develops certain beliefs, values, and preferences specific to the task itself which

*over time are generalized to other areas of life. . . . The theory . . .
constitutes an attempt to show in what way differences in task experience can help us to account for differences in what men believe,
prefer, and value.*[22]

In their usage, the term "attitude" includes these three outcomes
even though each is defined separately.

The underlying scheme is based on the assumptions that individuals gathered together to perform a task will adopt certain patterns
of behavior based on what they discover about the nature and
elements of the task and on the hypotheses they formulate for
going about it, and that they adopt those patterns of behavior
found to contribute most to the direct accomplishment of the
task and to the continuing joint efforts of those working on it.
Breer and Locke state:

*To the extent, for example, that a given task can be performed most
effectively when the individuals present cooperate closely with each
other, it is to be expected that in the course of working on the task
members will (1) become cognitively aware that cooperation is instrumental to task success, (2) behave in a cooperative fashion, (3) develop
a cathectic interest in cooperating with each other, and (4) establish
norms defining cooperation as a legitimate and expected form of behavior.*[23]

The inducement for the change in state of mind about the activity
derives from the gratifications, or their absence, obtained through
successful or unsuccessful performance.

The particular relevance of the Breer and Locke formulation to
understanding the connection between social setting and learning
lies in the generalization of experience; that is, with the formation of ideas more general than those bound to the specific task
experience. Thus: *". . . the orientations developed in response to a
given set of task attributes will be generalized to other task situations
and, through the process of induction, to the level of cultural beliefs,
preferences, and values* [according to a principle of similarity]." [24]
In one of the more dramatic empirical confirmations of their theory,
they found that group members working on tasks which were
accomplished more readily by an aggregate of individual efforts
than by collective effort become more favorably disposed to the
idea that individual efforts are more effective in performing tasks
in (1) small work groups (such as the ones they were in), (2) groups

NORMATIVE OUTCOMES OF SCHOOLING

in general, (3) families, (4) fraternities (in which group participants at the time of the study were not members), and (5) as a general principle or way of life. A parallel pattern of findings emerged from group experiences in which members worked on tasks accomplished more readily through collective rather than individual efforts. It is noteworthy, moreover, that the pattern of findings held up on four individual and four collective tasks; in other words, that they were not tied to any one specific task studied.[25]

Empirical support for the theory, as indicated by attitude changes in these five areas, and attitude generalization beyond the immediate task, raise questions about the principle of similarity underlying the process of generalization. Since one of the defining characteristics of norms is their situational specificity, the principle of similarity adequately accounts for the generalization of ideas beyond the task. However, it does not account for their generalization to some situations but not others. Breer and Locke may be correct in arguing that ideas at the cultural level can be traced to the fact that masses of individuals in a society have experiences in certain task situations, but it is also likely that experiences conducive to the generalization of ideas occur in situations that are also conducive to their specification.

If normative ideas are generalized from specific task experiences, as the Breer and Locke findings indicate that they are,[26] then the principle of generalization cannot be limited to similarity; generalization must occur in such a way that the ideas generated in a specific task situation apply to some circumstances but not to others. To illustrate this point: Earlier I indicated that children remained residential members of the family even during the years they left home to attend school, and that within families the members were expected to express affection toward each other and did so by and large. If children generalized their family experiences beyond the kinship setting, as Breer and Locke's subjects generalized their task experiences to fraternities (at least in their questionnaire responses), one would predict that they would express affection, for example, to schoolmates and teachers as they do to siblings and parents. This is not the case, however; not only is such behavior considered (normatively) inappropriate in school, but classrooms are organized in such a manner that it becomes very difficult to act in this way. To take another example: Pupils, both in the classroom and on athletic teams, are expected to perform the task at hand to the best of their ability; that is, to act according to achievement standards. In athletics, especially where coordinated team effort is required, individual achievement is both necessary and laudable up to the point where one member's desire to excel disrupts the team. Individual achievement is also encouraged in the classroom, but the pupil who strives to excel is not similarly disruptive because classroom activities are not usually designed as contributions to a collective product. Such a pupil may win the scorn of his classmates, but personal scorn and collective disruption are not the same.

These two examples indicate why the idea of generalization through the principle of similarity must be modified. In the second example, achievement is desirable in both situations, but the pupil must learn that the kind of achievement appropriate in one (in the classroom) is not so in the other (on a team); that is, beyond a certain point, the ideas acquired from one task experience lead to inappropriate behavior when generalized to another. In the first example, the properties of one social setting provide less opportunity for individuals to generalize the experience gained in another. This suggests that the change of setting represents one way of limiting the process of generalization, or, to put it more directly, to specify the type of behavior appropriate in each of the distinct situations. Actually, Breer and Locke's study design suggests one of the possible mechanisms by which the specification of norms may occur; namely, by group members performing individually tasks that are more effectively accomplished collectively, and vice versa. It may well be that when individuals gain experience over a sequence of situations, in some of which their task performance is successful and in others of which it is not, the overall impact of all their experiences is such that they learn where each particular principle of behavior is applicable and inapplicable. The necessity for considering both generalization and specification becomes clear if one considers an aggregation or sequence of experiences rather than one experience at a time.

Nowhere do Breer and Locke claim that the only way to create or change ideas is through task experience, yet their conceptual scheme as it stands contains no provision for variations in the structural properties of the settings in which individuals perform tasks. I would propose that, by taking into account both the nature of the task and the characteristics of the setting, it is possible to regulate the generation of ideas, generalizing them beyond and specifying them according to particular situations.

There is little basis for claiming that children learn principles of conduct by inferring them verbally from their experiences, yet it is not unreasonable to assume that learning occurs through some kind of symbolic process related to the use of language. The training program described by McClelland, for example, directly and explicitly utilizes the verbalization of principles to be acquired, and although the observations of Wheeler and the experiments of Breer and Locke do not refer directly to verbalization as the mechanism of learning, their interpretations implicitly assume that people make some kind of symbolic sense out of their surroundings even if they don't necessarily put it into words. Similarly, if I am correct in maintaining that schooling consists of a sequence of experiences from which pupils draw out the governing principles of conduct, then what is learned from these experiences is probably tied to psychological capacities related to children's use of language.

Although it is not possible to name some specific capacity that enables this inferential learning to occur, it should be of such a nature that children can symbolize in one way or another the similarities and differences between situations and their own place within them. Bernstein, in his studies of social class differences in the language usage of children, suggests that there are two basic types of language: public and formal. Public language, briefly, is characterized by short, simple, and concretely descriptive sentences, symbols expressed at a low level of generalization, restricted use of adjectives and adverbs, and spare use of impersonal pronouns.[27] Formal language has the opposite set of characteristics and is far better suited for expressing relationships between self and objects, making qualifications in what one says, and mediating between thought and feeling. Working class children, according to Bernstein, characteristically use the public language, while middle class children use the formal. But it is to the distinct advantage of the middle class child not only that he can handle the more flexible language but that he can understand and express himself in both languages, while the working class child tends to restrict his usage to the one. Bernstein contends:

The pressure within a middle-class social structure to intensify and verbalize an awareness of separateness and difference increases the significance of objects in the environment. Receptivity to a particular form of language structure determines the way relationships to objects are made and an orientation to a particular manipulation of words.[28]

The problem with the public language is that it lacks the symbolic equipment for communicating about the complex connections between persons, objects, time, and situations. It is, according to Bernstein, better suited to communication within solidary relationships among peers than in more complex relationships involving distinctions of status, and the verbal expressions necessary to convey the events of complex relationships are subject to distortion and misunderstanding when expressed in public language.

The distinction between public and formal language is most important in its implications for relationships of authority and the expression of thoughts within them. In particular, the content and justification of imperative statements are problematic. The public language does not contain a clear demarcation between the content and justification of commands and interdictions. When the reason for a command is not distinguished verbally from the statement of it, a challenge to the statement implies a challenge to the person who makes it:

The challenger immediately attacks the authority or legitimacy which is an attribute of the form of the relationship and this brings the social relationship into one of an affective type. However, if a formal language is used, reasons are separated from conclusions. The reasons can be challenged as inadequate or inappropriate which may initiate a second set of reasons or a development of the original set.[29]

The formal language, then, is better adapted to (1) keeping the substantive issue in an authority relationship open and (2) delaying, if not putting off entirely, the point at which the element of personal coercion enters. Moreover, Bernstein contends, statements of feeling and of qualification are more easily articulated in a formal language, while in public language they tend to remain implicit, being expressed more by nonverbal means. Formal language is sufficiently flexible to communicate statements of the public language, but the reverse is not true to nearly the same extent.

Bernstein's analysis of formal and public language grew out of his observations that middle class children tend to do better in school than working class children. He attributes this in part to the allegation that they differ in language usage. If he is correct, then it would appear that, whatever its empirical relationship to social class background happens to be, command of a formal language is more useful than command of a public language in making inferences from changing relationships between persons and circumstances and in establishing relationships of authority in which direct personal confrontations between superior and subordinate can be postponed or put off, both being constituent tasks of the process of schooling. Although the symbolic medium through which people infer principles of conduct from their experiences is not yet understood, Bernstein's work provides some especially fruitful conjectures because he has connected his propositions about language to the properties of the social situations in which that language ostensibly develops and in which it is used.

Earlier I maintained that one of the school's main contributions to learning lies in the area of social norms, and that a hypothetical answer to the question, "What is learned in school?" is: many things, including the traditionally recognized knowledge and skills, but also norms, or principles of conduct. It is true that other social agencies can provide climates conducive to the acquisition of norms, but no other agency (e.g., youth groups, families, churches, etc.) with some jurisdiction over children between the ages, roughly, of from six to eighteen, either does, nor seems as well suited to, produce the same set of norms produced in school, although other agencies do contribute to the process of their acquisition.

Evidence presented earlier lends support to the contention that the experiences schools afford their pupils, such as tasks, structural arrangements, constraints, sanctions, and opportunities for the generalization of ideas and investment of emotions, can produce normative changes. If schooling consisted simply of pupils reading books and teachers exhorting them about the right way to act, the conditions would not be adequate for the acquisition of norms.

Within the limitations of this discussion, it is not possible to settle the complex issues involved in determining the relationships among the knowledge of norms, acceptance of them as premises to govern action, and actual behavior oriented to them. Although these three elements are analytically independent, the existence of some empirical relationships among them must be assumed.

In more concrete form, the issues are clearly illustrated in McClelland's discussion of *n* Achievement (knowledge and motive, or norm) and entrepreneurship (behavior) in the context of economic development:

> . . . *we will try to discover what it is that a man does which makes theorists call him an entrepreneur. Then we shall check to see whether boys with high* n *Achievement in various countries of the world behave as an entrepreneur should before they have entered entrepreneurial positions and had a chance to be influenced by them. In this way we may hope to find out whether* n *Achievement leads people to behave in an entrepreneurial way, or whether an entrepreneurial position increases* n *Achievement, thereby leading to more vigorous entrepreneurial activity.*[30]

Here the relevant question is not whether the motive was acquired prior to occupying an entrepreneurial position or through experience in it, but whether behavior patterns can be generalized from one situation to another in the same way Breer and Locke have shown that attitudes are. That is, if the norm is learned and accepted in one situation and generalized to another, will individuals who conform to it in the first situation also conform to it in the second? The answer, of course, must be discovered empirically.

If pupils in school participate in activities that provide experiences conducive to the acquisition of norms (know the content of the norms, accept them as binding on themselves, and act in accordance with them in the appropriate situations), the question still remains: what norms? Again, only a hypothetical answer is possible at this point: the norms of *independence, achievement, universalism,* and *specificity.* To explain how schooling contributes to their acquisition is the task of the following chapter.

NOTES AND REFERENCES

1. In one near-encyclopedic volume on educational research, the instructional emphasis is most clearly illustrated. Nine of 23 long chapters are devoted to "Research on Teaching Various Grade Levels and Subject Matters." Six others deal with measurement both in regard to problems of measurement *per se* and of measuring particular types of educational outcomes (cognitive

and noncognitive). Two deal with the characteristics of teachers, two with methods and media, and one with social interaction in classrooms. The major preoccupations of educators and educational researchers are summarized in the following statement: "While it may or may not be true that the most important changes in the learner are those which may be described as cognitive, i.e., knowledge, problem-solving, higher mental processes, etc., it is true that these are the types of changes in students which most teachers do seek to bring about. These are the changes in learners which most teachers attempt to gauge in their own tests of progress and in their own final examinations. These, also, are the changes in the learners which are emphasized in the materials of instruction, in the interaction between teachers and learners, and in the reward system which the teachers and the schools employ." Benjamin S. Bloom, "Testing Cognitive Ability and Achievement," in N. L. Gage (ed.), *Handbook of Research on Teaching,* p. 379, Rand McNally and The American Educational Research Association, Chicago, (1963). There is a brief treatment of the characteristics of learning environments but with the primary emphasis on teaching techniques. George G. Stern, "Measuring Non-cognitive Variables in Research on Teaching," *ibid.,* pp. 425–433. Except for a brief excursion into sociometry, the same general approach is followed in the chapter on interaction. "We shall focus attention on the cognitive and affective interactions between teachers and learners, and learners and learners, and on the research that has been done to assess and quantify these acts." John Withal and W. W. Lewis, "Social Interaction in the Classroom," *ibid.,* p. 683.

Outside of the explicitly educational literature the most directly relevant body of research deals with changes in attitude and information. In a sequence of studies directed by Carl I. Hovland, many investigations include the characteristics of the audience, media of presentation, content expressed through the media, manner in which the content was communicated within each medium, and the impact of the communication on the audience. This summary description contains the main elements of the scheme although it does not do justice to the complexity and sophistication of the research. Most conspicuous by its absence in this series of investigations is any systematic treatment of the properties of the social settings in which these psychological changes occur. In effect, they are taken as nonproblematic.

2.   For a discussion of deliberate instruction in family settings, see Warren O. Hagstrom, "A Study of Deliberate Instruction within Family Units," unpublished manuscript, University of Wisconsin, June, 1965.

3.   Warren O. Hagstrom, *ibid.*, pp. 25–41.

4.   Lest there be any doubt about it, see Claude Brown, *Manchild in the Promised Land,* Macmillan, New York (1965).

5.   The empirical problems in identifying norms in a given situation are beyond the scope of this discussion. Suffice it to say that identifying them requires that one consider at least the following: verbal statements, behavior, situation, and emotional expressions, none of which is sufficient when taken alone.

6.   The distinction is illustrated in the following quotation: "Presumably, a preference for sons is a value, but it says nothing concrete concerning parental conduct and it has no sanctions. A norm, on the other hand, says that a given line of conduct must, or should, be followed." Judith Blake and Kingsley Davis, "Norms, Values, and Sanctions," in Robert E. L. Faris (ed.), *Handbook of Modern Sociology,* p. 460, Rand McNally, Chicago (1964). It is difficult to make a hard and fast distinction between values and norms. In regard to this quotation: if the statement had read, ". . . a preference for children . . . ," the preference for sons might be called a norm because it is more specific. Blake and Davis continue: "Thus a preference for sons in the United States does not mean that female infanticide is permitted or that boys are given more clothes," *ibid.,* p. 460. But how specific must the description of conduct be to distinguish between a norm and a value? There is no unequivocal answer to this question, but clearly one can look for a description of specific behavior as a rule of thumb, one that could reasonably exclude a verb as vague as 'prefer' in the context of the above quotation.

7.   For a conceptual discussion of this problem, see Gross, Mason, and McEachern, *Explorations in Role Analysis*, pp. 281–318, John Wiley and Sons, New York (1958). Blake and Davis put the issue as follows: "The fact that some norms are uncontrollable elements of the situation in which the individual must try to conform to other norms means that one important source of unintentionally deviant behavior may be located, paradoxically, in normative demands themselves." Judith Blake and Kingsley Davis, "Norms, Values, and Sanctions," p. 469.

8. Stouffer, in a study of norms about cheating on college exams, found that students, asked to imagine themselves in the role of proctors, would sanction cheaters conditionally. In its explicit form, the norm against cheating is a flat proscription, and university policy recognizes no exceptions. Stouffer found that proctors said they would take the following circumstances into account in their action: whether the cheater was a friend or an ordinary student; whether the proctor's action would come to the attention of the administration or to that of fellow students. The subjects of the study varied in the punitiveness of their hypothetical proctoring depending on these prevailing conditions. Samuel A. Stouffer, "An Analysis of Conflicting Social Norms," *American Sociological Review* 14, No. 6, 707–717 (1949).

9. Several observers have been concerned with the problematic nature of social norms and the relationship of behavior to them. For example: "Although role conformity may be approached through the theorem of institutional integration, that is, that individuals carry out institutional tasks because they have been reared to want to do so, this theorem is only an orientation and not a precise hypothesis. Many do not discharge their responsibilities while wanting to do so. The road to hell is paved with good intentions: conformity to a set of norms is not a simple function of norm commitment." William J. Goode, "Norm Commitment and Conformity to Role-Status Obligations," *American Journal of Sociology* **66**, No. 3, 251 (1960). "It does not seem necessary to assume that 'internalization' involves a blocking out of deviant motives such as would take place in sublimation and repression. Rather, we simply assume that *in the face of* temptation, one source of resistance to acting out deviant motivation in deviant behavior lies in the person's commitment to norms proscribing the behavior, and in his ability to symbolize significantly to himself the moral reasons for not succumbing. . . . Internalization is clearly not always successful as a source of self-imposed inhibition to deviant behavior. Consequently, there is wide latitude for the investigation of sources of *variation* in the effectiveness of internalization as a control mechanism." Judith Blake and Kingsley Davis, "Norms, Values, and Sanctions," pp. 478–479. And Carlin, in his study of the New York City Bar, distinguishes between the degree of acceptance of norms (measured by lawyers' disapproval of unethical action, the saliency they ascribe to norms, and estimates of the prevalence of unethical practices), and adherence to norms (a behavioral component). Jerome E. Carlin, *Lawyers' Ethics*, pp. 47–52, Russell Sage Foundation, New York (1966).

10. William J. Goode, "Norm Commitment and Conformity to Role-Status Obligations," p. 253.

11. David C. McClelland, "Toward a Theory of Motive Acquisition," *American Psychologist* **20**, No. 5, 321–333 (1965).

12. The ability of persons to verbalize the content of norms is neither necessary nor sufficient for determining empirically whether they accept them; moreover, a verbal statement may or may not serve as an adequate index of norm acceptance. The word "internalization" is customarily used to refer to what I have called norm acceptance. The usage of "internalization" varies but often refers to a premise so thoroughly accepted that the person *may* not be able to verbalize it. The existence of internalized norms must be inferred from the emotional reactions that follow behavioral deviations from them. I use the term "acceptance" to avoid the overly-limited, nonverbal connotation that often attaches to "internalization." For a discussion of the conceptual and methodological problems related to internalization, see Wesley Allinsmith, "The Learning of Moral Standards," in Daniel R. Miller and Guy E. Swanson, (eds.), *Inner Conflict and Defense,* pp. 141–176, Henry Holt, New York (1960); and Justin Aronfreed and Arthur Reber, "Internalized Behavioral Suppression and the Timing of Social Punishment," *Journal of Personality and Social Psychology* **1**, No. 1, 3–5 (1965) for a discussion of emotion as it pertains to internalization.

13. David C. McClelland, "Toward a Theory of Motive Acquisition," p. 322.

14. David C. McClelland, *ibid.,* p. 325.

15. David C. McClelland, *ibid.,* p. 326.

16. David C. McClelland, *ibid.,* p. 325.

17. David C. McClelland, *ibid.,* p. 326.

18. See, for example, Howard S. Becker, *et al, Boys in White,* University of Chicago Press, Chicago (1961); Theodore M. Newcomb, *Personality and Social Change,* Dryden Press, New York (1943); and William Caudill, *The Psychiatric Hospital as a Small Society,* Harvard University Press, Cambridge (1958).

19. Stanton Wheeler, "The Structure of Formally Organized Socialization Settings," in Orville G. Brim, Jr., and Stanton Wheeler, *Socialization After Childhood,* p. 53, John Wiley and Sons, New York (1966).

20. Stanton Wheeler, *ibid.,* p. 61. The following are examples of the four resulting types: (1) Individual-Disjunctive, oldest child in a family; (2) Collective-Disjunctive, summer training institute; (3) Individual-Serial, new occupant of a job previously held by another person; and (4) Collective-Serial, school, prison, mental hospital.

21. Stanton Wheeler, *ibid.,* p. 73; my emphases. Even though Wheeler does not spell out the analogous implications of school composition, the parallel with the school is clear, as illustrated earlier in this book. People learn something simply from their social experiences (for example, the collective characteristics of those with whom they come into contact) independently of the "curriculum": in school, the subjects of instruction; in prison, the "criminal value system" and the deliberate efforts toward rehabilitation.

22. Paul E. Breer and Edwin A. Locke, *Task Experience as a Source of Attitudes,* p. 10, The Dorsey Press, Homewood, Ill. (1965). As they use the terms, beliefs refer to existential statements about the nature of things; preferences to the liking or disliking of objects; and values to judgments made on moral or normative grounds. *Ibid.,* p. 7.

23. Paul E. Breer and Edwin C. Locke, *ibid.,* p. 13.

24. Paul E. Breer and Edwin C. Locke, *ibid.,* p. 15; my emphasis. "We have suggested that the greater the similarity between two task situations, the more likely it is that orientations developed in one situation will generalize to the other. This is what we have called 'lateral generalization,' i.e., generalization from one specific stimulus-complex to another. We have hypothesized that generalization also proceeds vertically, i.e., along an inductive chain from the specific to the increasingly abstract." *Ibid.,* p. 35.

25. Paul E. Breer and Edwin C. Locke, *ibid.,* pp. 138–161. The findings for small work groups, groups in general, and way of life represented vertical generalization; those for family and fraternity, horizontal generalization.

26. Breer and Locke worded their attitude questions so that they contained statements of belief, preference, and value (the latter subsuming the concept of norm). For an example of a normative item: "Family tasks should be arranged so individual members can do as many things as possible on their own with a minimum of joint co-operation." Paul E. Breer and Edwin C. Locke, *ibid.,* p. 159. They found that ideas in all three attitude areas changed in the predicted direction, indicating that the same task experiences were efficacious in changing the three different types of ideas.

27. Basil Bernstein, "A Public Language: Some Sociological Implications of A Linguistic Form," *British Journal of Sociology* **10,** No. 4, 311–326 (1959). A more complete definition appears on p. 311.

28. Basil Bernstein, "Some Sociological Determinants of Perception," *British Journal of Sociology* **9,** No. 2, 165 (1958).

29. Basil Bernstein, "A Public Language: . . ." p. 314.

30. David C. McClelland, *The Achieving Society,* p. 206, Van Nostrand, Princeton (1961).

CHAPTER FIVE

THE CONTRIBUTION OF SCHOOLING TO THE LEARNING OF NORMS: INDEPENDENCE, ACHIEVEMENT, UNIVERSALISM, AND SPECIFICITY

Generally speaking . . . a teacher must balance a concern with specific accomplishments with some concern for a state of well-being: he has to keep a relatively "happy" class which "learns." But a class is more than a collection of individuals. The teacher always has to manage children in groups. His acts towards individuals must somehow be interpreted either as expressions of general rules or of a particular circumstance. In the latter case he must draw the further line between legitimate special treatment and favouritism. He must teach the relegation of private needs as well as their occasional relevance.

Kaspar D. Naegele, "Clergymen, Teachers, and Psychiatrists: . . ."

In speaking of these four ideas as norms, I mean that individuals accept them as legitimate standards for governing their own conduct in the appropriate situations. Specifically, they accept the obligations to (1) act by themselves (unless collaborative effort is called for), and accept personal responsibility for their conduct and accountability for its consequences; (2) perform tasks actively and master the environment according to certain standards of excellence; and (3) acknowledge the rights of others to treat them as members of categories (4) on the basis of a few discrete characteristics rather than on the full constellation of them that represent the whole person. I treat these four norms because they are integral parts of public and occupational life in industrial societies, or institutional realms adjacent to the school.

In earlier parts of this book, I have discussed only the pre-adult phases of socialization, which occur in the family of orientation and in the school. In one sense, at least for men, full adult status requires occupational employment, and one of the outcomes of schooling is employability. The capacity to hold a job involves not only adequate physical capacities (in part the outcome of biological maturation), but also the appropriate intellectual and psychological skills to cope with the demands of work. The requirements of job-holding are multifarious; however, most occupations require, among other things, that individuals take personal responsibility for the completion and quality of their work and individual accountability for its shortcomings, and that they perform their tasks to the best of their ability.

Public life extends beyond occupational employment. Even though people work as members of occupational categories, and in association with others as clients, patients, customers, parishioners, students, and so on, they also have nonoccupational identities as voters, communicants, petitioners, depositors, applicants, and creditors (to name just a few), in which people are similarly classified according to one primary characteristic, irrespective of how they differ otherwise.

Goode observes:

The prime social characteristic of modern industrial enterprise is that the individual is ideally given a job on the basis of his ability to fulfill its demands, and that this achievement is evaluated universalistically; the same standards apply to all who hold the same job.[1]

Industrially oriented societies tend to have occupational systems based on normative principles different from those of kinship units. Many observers, recognizing that individuals must undergo psychological changes of considerable magnitude in order to make the transition from family of orientation to economic employment,[2] have noted (but at the same time understated) the contribution of schooling. Eisenstadt, for example, in an otherwise penetrating analysis of age-grouping, restricts his treatment of the school's contribution to that of "... *adapting the psychological (and to some extent also physiological) learning potential of the child to the various skills and knowledges which must be acquired by him.*" [3] Eisenstadt's emphasis is too narrowly limited to those cognitive outcomes of schooling related to instrumental knowledge.

Furthermore, while stressing the transition between family and occupation, most writers have largely ignored the contribution of schooling to the development of psychological capacities necessary for participating in other (noneconomic) segments of society. It is my contention that the social experiences available to pupils in schools, by virtue of the nature and sequence of their structural arrangements, provide opportunities for children to learn norms characteristic of several facets of adult public life, occupation being but one.

The social properties of schools are such that pupils, by coping with the sequence of classroom tasks and situations, are more likely to learn the principles (i.e., social norms) of independence, achievement, universalism, and specificity than if they had remained full-time members of the household. Although I have spoken thus far only of the similarities and differences between the family and the school, the nature of that comparison is largely determined by the character of public institutions, in particular the economy and the polity. Schools, that is to say, form one of several institutional linkages between the household and the public sphere of adult life, a linkage organized around stages of the life cycle in industrial societies. There is substantial evidence that conduct in the family and conduct on the job are governed by contrasting normative principles. From this we can imply that if the education of children were carried on primarily within the jurisdiction of the family, the nature of experiences available in that setting would not provide conditions appropriate for acquiring those capacities that enable people to participate competently in the public realm.

It is not inevitable that schools should provide such an institutional linkage, but the fact of the matter is that they do, even though there are other candidates for the job. Mass media, for example, might perform a comparable knowledge-dispensing function, and if their potentialities for effecting more profound psychological changes were plumbed, they might constitute an agency sufficiently potent to bring about changes in principles of conduct. The media have not yet proved up to the job, however, perhaps in part because children's early experiences in the family predispose them to be responsive to human agents, and the media do not provide such agents. In fact, much research on the impact of mass media points to the importance of human links in the chain from source to audience. Occupational apprenticeship might be an acceptable substitute for the schools; it has the human element and is directly related to occupational employment, one of the main locations of men's engagement in the public sphere of industrial society. Apprenticeship, however, like the media, has its own liabilities, one of which is that it continues relationships of dependency (not of child on parent, but of worker on employer), and those relationships are often found to be incompatible with many of the institutional demands of public life. Since the media and apprenticeship arrangements do not exhaust the possibilities, and since I am not trying to demonstrate the inevitability of schools, the impact of schooling remains to be explained, because schools are what we have. I turn, then, to a discussion of how the experiences of schooling contribute to the acquisition of the four norms in question.

INDEPENDENCE

One answer to the question, "What is learned in school?" is that pupils learn to acknowledge that there are tasks they must do alone, and to do them that way. Along with this self-imposed obligation goes the idea that others have a legitimate right to expect such independent behavior under certain circumstances.[4] Independence has a widely acknowledged though not unequivocal meaning. In using it here I refer to a cluster of meanings: doing things on one's own, being self-reliant, accepting personal responsibility for one's behavior, acting self-sufficiently,[5] and handling tasks with which, *under different circumstances,* one can rightfully expect the help of others. The pupil, when in school, is separated from family members who have customarily provided help, support, and sustenance, persons on whom he has long been dependent.

A constellation of classroom characteristics, teacher actions, and pupil actions shape experiences in which the norm of independence is learned. In addition to the fact that school children are removed from persons with whom they have already formed strong relationships of dependency, the sheer size of a classroom assemblage limits each pupil's claim to personal contact with the teacher, and more so at the secondary levels than at the elementary. This numerical property of classrooms reduces pupils' opportunities for establishing new relationships of dependency with adults and for receiving help from them.

Parents expect their children to act independently in many situations, but teachers are more systematic in expecting pupils to adhere to standards of independence in performing academic tasks. There are at least two additional aspects of classroom operation that bear directly on learning the norm of independence: rules about cheating and formal testing. Let us consider cheating first. The word itself is condemnatory in its reference to illegal and immoral acts. Most commonly, attention turns to how much cheating occurs, who cheats, and why. But these questions, while of great importance elsewhere, are of no concern here. My interest is in a different problem: to what types of conduct is the pejorative "cheating" assigned?

In school, cheating pertains primarily to instructional activities and usually refers to acts in which two or more parties participate when the unaided action of only one is expected. Illegal or immoral acts such as stealing and vandalism, whether carried out by individuals or groups, are not considered cheating because they have no direct connection with the central academic core of school activities. Nor is joint participation categorically proscribed; joint effort is called cooperation or collusion depending on the teacher's prior definition of the task.

Cheating takes many forms, most of which involve collective effort. A parent and a child may collaborate to produce homework; two pupils can pool their wisdom (or ignorance, as the case may be) in the interest of passing an examination. In both cases the parties join deliberately, although deliberateness is not essential to the definition; one pupil can copy from another without the latter knowing. In the case of plagiarism, of course, the second party is not a person at all, but information compiled by another. The use of crib notes, perhaps a limiting case, involves no collusion; it consists, rather, of an illegitimate form of help. These are the main forms of school cheating, but there are many variations, routine to exotic. Thus actions called cheating are those closely tied to the instructional goals of the school and usually involve assisted performance when unaided performance is expected. As one observer put it: Pupils ". . . *must learn to distinguish between cooperating and cheating."* [6]

The irony of cheating *in school* is that the same kinds of acts are considered morally acceptable and even commendable in other situations. It is praiseworthy for one friend to assist another in distress, or for a parent to help a child; and if one lacks the information to do a job, the resourceful thing is to look it up. In effect, many school activities called cheating are the customary forms of support and assistance in the family and among friends.

In one obvious sense, school rules against cheating are designed to establish the content of moral standards. In another sense, the school attaches the stigma of immorality to certain types of behavior for social as distinct from ethical reasons; namely, to change the character of prevailing social relationships in which children are involved. In the case of homework, the school, in effect, attempts to redefine the relationship between parents and children by proscribing one kind of parental support, which is not a problem in other circumstances. The teacher has no direct control over parents but tries to influence them at a distance by asking their adherence to a principle clothed in moral language whose violations are punishable. The line between legitimate parental support (encouraged when it takes the form of parents stressing the importance of school and urging their children to do well) and collusion is unclear, but by morally proscribing parental intervention beyond a certain point, the teacher attempts to limit the child's dependence on family members in doing his school work. In other words, he expects the pupil to work independently. The same argument applies to pupils and their friends; the teacher attempts to eliminate those parts of friendship that make it difficult or impossible for him to discover what a pupil can do on his own. In relationships with kin and friends, the customary sources of support in times of adversity, the school intervenes by restricting solidarity and, in the process, determines what the pupil can accomplish unaided. The pupil, for his part, discovers which of his actions he is held accountable for individually within the confines of tasks set by the school.

This argument is indirectly supported by the comparison between schooling and the occupational employment for which school is intended as preparation. The question here is the sense in which school experience is preparatory. Usually workers are not restricted in seeking help on problems confronting them; on the contrary, many occupations provide resources specifically intended to be helpful: arrangements for consultation, libraries, access to more experienced colleagues, and so on. Only in rare situations are people expected not to enlist the aid of family and friends in matters pertaining to work where that aid is appropriate. In other words, activities on the job, directly analogous to school work, do not carry comparable restrictions. However, people in their occupational activities are required to accept individual responsibility and accountability for the performance of assigned and self-initiated tasks. To the extent that the school contributes to the development of independence, the preparation lies more in the development of a psychological disposition to act independently than to perform a certain range of tasks without help.

Second, as to testing, and particularly the use of achievement tests; most important for independence are the social conditions designed for the *administration* of tests, not their content or format. By and large, pupils are tested under more or less rigorously controlled conditions. At one end of the spectrum, formal standardized tests are administered most stringently; pupils are physically separated, and the testing room is patrolled by proctors whose job is to discover contraband and to guarantee that no communication occurs, these arrangements being designed so that each examination paper represents independent work. At the other end, some testing situations are more informal, less elaborately staged, although there is almost always some provision to ensure that each pupil's work represents the product of only his own efforts.

Testing represents an approach to establishing the norm of independence, which is different from the proscription against cheating even though both are designed to reduce the likelihood of joint effort. Whereas the rules against cheating are directed toward delineating the form of appropriate behavior, the restrictions built into the testing situation provide physical constraints intended to guarantee that teachers will receive samples of the work pupils do unassisted. Actually, unless they stipulate otherwise, teachers expect pupils to do most of their everyday work by themselves; daily assignments provide the opportunities for and practice in independent work. Tests, because they occur at less frequent intervals than ordinary assignments, cannot provide comparably frequent opportunities; by the elaborate trappings of their administration, particularly with college entrance exams, and the anxiety they provoke, they symbolize the magnitude of the stakes.

It may be objected that in emphasizing independence I have ignored cooperation, since an important item on the school agenda is the instruction of pupils in the skills of working with others. Teachers do assign work to groups and expect a collaborative product, and to this extent they require the subordination of individual to collective efforts, but judging the product according to collective standards is another question.

To evaluate the contribution of each member of a working team, the teacher must either judge the quality of each one's work, in effect relying on the standard of independence, or rate each contribution according to the quality of the total product. The latter procedure rests on the assumption that each member has contributed equally, an untenable assumption if one member has carried the rest or if a few members have carried a weak sister. That occurrences of this kind are usually considered "unfair" suggests the normative priority of independence and the simple fact of life in industrial societies; i.e., that institutions of higher learning and employers want to know how well each person can do and put constraints on the schools in order to find out. Thus, although the school provides opportunities for pupils to gain experience in cooperative situations, in the last analysis it is the individual assessment that counts.

ACHIEVEMENT

Pupils come to accept the premise that they should perform their tasks the best they can, and act accordingly. The concept of achievement, like independence, has several referents. It usually denotes activity and mastery, making an impact on the environment rather than fatalistically accepting it, and competing against some standard of excellence. Analytically, the concept should be distinguished from independence, since, among other differences, achievement criteria can apply to activities performed collectively.

Much of the recent literature treats achievement in the context of child-rearing within the family as if achievement motivation were primarily a product of parental behavior.[7] Even though there is reason to believe that early childhood experiences in the family do contribute to its development, classroom experiences also contribute through teachers' use of resources beyond those ordinarily at the command of family members.

Classrooms are organized around a set of core activities in which a teacher assigns tasks to pupils and evaluates and compares the quality of their work. In the course of time, pupils differentiate themselves according to how well they perform a variety of tasks, most of which require the use of symbolic skills. Achievement standards are not limited in applicability to the classroom nor is their content restricted to the cognitive areas. Schools afford opportunities for participation in a variety of extra-curricular activities, most conspicuously athletics, but also music, dramatics, and a bewildering array of club and small group activities serving individual interests and talents.

The direct relevance of classroom work in providing task experience judged by achievement criteria is almost self-evident; the experience is built into the assignment-performance-evaluation sequence of the work. Less evident, however, is the fact that these activities force pupils to cope with various degrees of success and failure, both of which can be psychologically problematic. Consistently successful performance requires that pupils deal with the consequences of their own excellence in a context of peer equality in nonacademic areas. For example, they confront the dilemma inherent in having surpassed their age-mates in some respects while depending on their friendship and support in others, particularly in out-of-school social activities. The classroom provides not only the achievement experience itself but by-products of it, taking the form of the dilemma just described.

Similarly, pupils whose work is consistently poor not only must participate in achievement activities leading to their failure, they must also experience living with that failure. They adopt various modes of coping with this, most of which center around maintaining personal self-respect in the face of continuing assaults upon it. Probably a minority succeed or fail consistently; a majority, most likely, do neither one consistently, but nonetheless worry about not doing well. Schooling, then, assures most pupils the experiences of both winning and losing, and to the extent that they gain some modicum of gratification from academic activities, it teaches them to approach their work in a frame of mind conducive to achievement. At the same time they learn how to cope, in a variety of ways and more or less well, with success and failure.

Failure is perhaps the more difficult condition with which to cope because it requires acknowledgment that the premise of achievement, to which failure itself can be attributed in part, is a legitimate principle by which to govern one's actions. Yet situations that constrain people to live with personal failure are endemic to industrial societies in which many facets of public life are based on achievement principles; political defeat and occupational nonpromotion being two cases in point.

As suggested earlier, the school provides a broad range of experiences other than those restricted to the classroom and academic in nature; these experiences are also based on achievement criteria but differ in several important respects. Alternatives to academic performance give the pupil a chance to succeed in achievement-oriented activities even though he may not be able to do well in the classroom.

How these alternative activities differ from those of the classroom is as important as the fact that they do so differ, as evidenced by the case of athletics. Competitive sports resemble classroom activities in that both provide participants with the chance to demonstrate individual excellence. However, the former—and this is more true of team than individual sports—permit collective responsibility for defeat, whereas the latter by and large allow only individual responsibility for failure. That is to say, the chances of receiving personal gratification for success are at least as great in sports as in the classroom, while the assault on personal self-respect for failure is potentially less intense. Athletics should not be written off as a manifestation of mere adolescent nonintellectualism, as recent writers have treated it.[8] I do not suggest that athletics has an as yet undiscovered intellectual richness; rather that its contribution should not be viewed simply in terms of intellectuality. Wilkinson, in talking about athletics in the British public schools, makes a similar argument, not so much in terms of mitigating the psychological consequences of achievement for individuals as in striking a balance between competition and social cooperation:

On the football field and on the river, the public school taught its boys to compete, not so much in personal contests, as in struggles between groups—between teams, houses, and schools. . . . They preserved middle-class morality and energy, but they adapted these to the needs of the public servant,[9]

so important, according to Wilkinson, in establishing the ethic that private privilege meant public duty.

A similar contention holds for music and dramatics; both provide the potentiality for individual accomplishment and recognition without the persistent, systematic, and potentially corrosive evaluation typical of the classroom. Finally, in various club activities based on interest and talent, a pupil can do the things he is good at in the company of others who share an appreciation for them. In all these situations, either the rigors of competition and judgment characteristic of the classroom are mitigated, or the activity in question has its own built-in source of support and personal protection, not to the same extent as in the family, but more than is available in the crucible of the classroom.

The school provides a wider variety of achievement experiences than does the family, but it also has fewer resources for supporting and protecting pupils' self-respect in the face of failure. As pupils proceed through successive school levels, the rigors of achievement increase, at least for those who continue along the main academic line. Moreover, at the secondary levels the number of activities governed according to achievement principles increases as does the variety of these activities. As preparation for adult public life in which the application of these principles is widespread, schooling contributes to personal development in assuring that the majority of pupils not only will have performed tasks according to the achievement standard, but that they will have had experience in an expanding number of situations in which activities are organized according to it.

UNIVERSALISM AND SPECIFICITY

Unlike independence and achievement, universalism and specificity are not commonly regarded as good things. Parents and teachers admonish children to act independently and do their work well; few of them support the idea that people should willingly acknowledge their similarity to one another in specifically categorical terms while ignoring their obvious differences; that is, in a sense, denying their own individuality.

Ideologically, social critics have deplored the impersonal, ostensibly dehumanizing, aspects of categorization, a principle widely believed to lie at the heart of the problem of human alienation; the attachment of man to machine, the detachment of man from man. Often ignored, however, is the connection between this principle and the idea of fairness, or equity. Seen from this vantage point, categorization is widely regarded as a good thing, especially when contrasted to nepotism, favoritism, and arbitrariness. People resent the principle when they think they have a legitimate reason to receive special consideration, and when their individuality appears to vanish by being "processed." Yet when a newcomer breaks into a long queue of patiently waiting people instead of proceeding to the end of the line, they usually condemn him for acting unfairly (for not following the standard rule for all newcomers to a line). They do *not* react by expressing any sense of their own alienation, since they accept the same categorical principle as binding on themselves. In other words, this is not the occasion to proclaim one's individuality, but to act like everybody else and be sure they do likewise. The contrasts between the two dualities (individuality and dehumanization, fairness and special privilege) are similarly predicated on the principles of universalism and specificity; people differ in their posture toward each duality according to ideological position, situation, and, more cynically, in their conception of self-interest.

The concepts of universalism and specificity have been formulated most comprehensively by Parsons, though only part of his formulation is directly germane to this discussion. As part of his concern with social systems, Parsons views universalism as one horn of a dilemma (the other being particularism) in role definition; under what circumstances does the occupant of one social position govern his actions by adopting one standard or another when dealing with

CONTRIBUTION OF SCHOOLING TO THE LEARNING OF NORMS

the occupant of another social position? My concern, however, is not with a selection among alternative, conflicting standards, but with the conditions under which individuals learn to impose the standards of universalism and specificity on themselves and to act accordingly.

Defining the central theme of universalism raises problems because the term has been assigned a variety of meanings, not all of them clear.[10] The relevant distinction here is whether individuals are treated in terms of their membership in categories or as special cases. In one respect or another an individual can always be viewed as a member of one or more categories, universalistically; he is viewed particularistically if, considering his similarity to others in the same category, he still receives special treatment. As Blau puts it:

An attribute is defined as a universalistic standard if persons, regardless of their own characteristics, direct a disproportionate number of their positive (or negative) evaluations to others with a certain characteristic. An attribute is defined as a particularistic standard if persons tend to direct their positive (or, in special cases, negative) evaluations to others whose characteristics are like their own.[11]

The treatment of others does not become more particularistic as an increasing number of categories is taken into account. If age, sex, religion, ethnicity, and the like are considered, all examples of general categories, treatment is still categorical in nature because it is oriented to categorical similarities and not to what is special about the person. Thus, *"A man's orientation toward his family,"* according to Blau, *"is considered particularistic because it* singles out for special attention *the members of an ingroup, rather than persons with a certain attribute regardless of whether it makes them part of his ingroup or not."*[12]

The norm of specificity is easily confused with universalism despite its distinctiveness. It refers to the scope of one person's interest in another; to the obligation to confine one's interest to a narrow range of characteristics and concerns, or to extend them to include a broad range.[13] The notion of relevance is implicit; the characteristics and concerns that should be included within the range, whether broad or narrow, are those considered relevant in terms of the activities in which the persons in question are involved. Doctors and storekeepers, for example, differ in the scope of the interest they have in the persons seeking their services, but the content of their interests also varies according to the nature of the needs and desires of those persons.

It is my contention that what the school contributes to the acceptance by children of those norms that penetrate many areas of public life is critical, because children's pre-school experience in the family is weighted heavily on the side of special treatment and parental consideration of the whole child. To say that children learn the norm of universalism means that they come to accept being treated by others as members of categories (in addition to being treated as special cases, as in the family).

Categorization

Schools provide a number of experiences that families cannot readily provide because of limitations in their social composition and structure. One such experience is the systematic establishment and demarcation of membership categories. First, by assigning all pupils in a classroom the same or similar tasks to perform, teachers in effect make them confront the same set of demands. Even if there are variations in task content, class members still confront the same teacher and the obligations he imposes. Second, parity of age creates a condition of homogeneity according to developmental stage, a rough equalization of pupil capacities making it possible for teachers to assign similar tasks. Third, through the process of yearly promotion from grade to grade, pupils cross the boundaries separating one age category from another. With successive boundary crossings comes the knowledge that each age-grade category is associated with a particular set of circumstances (e.g., teachers, difficulty of tasks, subject matter studied). Moreover, pupils learn the relationship between categories and how their present position relates to past and future positions by virtue of having experienced the transitions between them. In these three ways, the grade (more specifically the classroom within the grade) with its age-homogeneous membership and clearly demarcated boundaries provides a basis for categorical grouping that the family cannot readily duplicate. Most important, the experiences of membership in a group of age-equals and repeated boundary crossings makes it possible for pupils to acquire a relativity of perspective, a capacity to view their own circumstances from other vantage points that they themselves have occupied.[14]

Although each child holds membership in the category "children" at home, parents, in raising them, tend to take age differences into account and thereby accentuate the uniqueness of each child's circumstances, thus belying in some measure the categorical aspects of "childhood." However, even if the category "children" breaks into its age-related components within the family, it remains intact when children compare themselves with friends and neighbors of similar age. In typical situations of this kind, children inform their parents that friends of the same age have greater privileges or fewer responsibilities than they. Parents, if they cannot actually equalize the circumstances, often explain or justify the disparity by pointing to the special situation of the neighbor family; they have more money, fewer children, a bigger house. Whatever the reason, that is, parents point out the uniqueness of family circumstances and thereby emphasize the particularities of each child's situation. The school, in contrast, provides the requisite circumstances for making comparisons among pupils in categorical rather than particular terms.

Another school experience fostering the establishment of social categories is the re-equalization of pupils by means of the high school track system after they have differentiated themselves through academic achievement in the lower grades, a mechanism that minimizes the likelihood of teachers having to deal with special cases. Teachers with a variegated batch of pupils must adopt more individualized methods of instruction than those whose pupils are similar in their level of achievement. In so doing, they partially recreate a kinship-type of relationship with pupils, treating segments of the class differently according to differences in capacity, much as parents treat their children differently according to age-related capacities.

As far as level is concerned, the high school is a better place to acquire the principle of universalism than the lower school levels because pupils within each track, who are of roughly similar capacity, move from classroom to classroom, in each one receiving instruction in a different subject area by a different teacher. They discover that over a range of activities, they are treated alike and that relatively uniform demands and criteria of evaluation are applied to them. Thus they learn which differences in experience are subordinated to the principle of categorization. The elementary classroom, oriented more to instruction in different subjects by a single teacher, does not provide the necessary variations in persons and subjects for a clear-cut demonstration of the categorical principle.

Persons and Positions

Although the idea of categorization is central to the norm of universalism, it has additional and derivative aspects. One is the crucial distinction, widely relevant in industrial societies, between the person and the social position he occupies. Individuals are often expected to treat one another according to their social position, rather than according to their individual identity. Schooling contributes to the capacity to make the distinction (and to the obligation to do so) by making it possible for pupils to discover that different individuals occupying a single social position often act in ways that are attached to the position rather than to the different persons filling it. Even though all members of a given classroom find themselves in the same circumstances (they are about equal in age and roughly resemble each other in social characteristics related to residence), they still differ in many respects: sex, race, religion, ethnicity, and physical characteristics being among the most obvious. Their situation, therefore, provides the experience of finding that common interests and shared circumstances are assigned a priority that submerges obvious personal differences. The same contention holds for adults. Male and female adults are found in both school and family settings; in school, pupils can discover that an increasingly large number of different adults of both sexes can occupy the same position, that of "teacher." This discovery is not as easily made in the family because it is not possible to determine definitively whether "parent" represents two positions, one occupied by a male, the other by a female, or a single position with two occupants differing in sex. Children are not left completely without clues in this matter since they do have other adult relatives who can be seen as distinct persons occupying the same position: aunts, uncles, grandparents, and the like. Yet even extended families do not provide the frequent and systematic comparisons characteristic of the schools. Schooling, in other words, enables pupils to distinguish between persons and the social positions they occupy (a capacity crucially important in both occupational and political life) by placing them in situations in which the membership of each position is varied in its composition and the similarities between persons in a single position are made evident.

Specificity

The school provides structural arrangements more conducive to the acquisition of the norm of specificity than does the family. First, since the number of persons and the ratio between adults and nonadults is much larger in classrooms than in the household, the school provides large social aggregates in which pupils can form many casual associations (in addition to their close friendships) in which they invest but a small portion of themselves. As both the size and heterogeneity of the student body increase at each successive level, the opportunities for these somewhat fragmented social contacts increase and diversify. The relative shallowness and transiency of these relationships increase the likelihood that pupils will have experiences in which the fullness of their individuality is *not* involved, as it tends to be in their relationships among kin and close friends.

Second, on leaving the elementary school and proceeding through the departmentalized secondary levels, pupils form associations with teachers who have a progressively narrowing and specialized interest in them. (This comes about both because of subject matter specialization itself and because the number of pupils each teacher faces in the course of a day grows larger.) Although it is true that children, as they grow older, tend to form more specific relationships with their parents (symptomatically, this trend manifests itself in adolescents' complaints of parental invasions of privacy), the resources of the school far exceed those of the family in providing the social basis for the establishment of relationships in which only narrow segments of personality are invested.

Equity

An additional facet of universalism is the principle of equity, or fairness (I use the terms interchangeably). When children compare their lot—their gains and losses, rewards and punishments, privileges and responsibilities—with that of others and express dissatisfaction about their own, they have begun to think in terms of equity; their punishments are too severe, chores too onerous, allowance too small compared to those of siblings and friends. Children's comparisons with siblings, who are almost always different in age, usually prompt parents to try to resolve the sensed inequities by equalizing age hypothetically. "If you were as young as he, you wouldn't have to shovel the walk either." "He is only a child and doesn't know any better." The pained questions to which these statements are replies are familiar enough.

Writers who have discussed problems of equity and inequity have usually done so in order to identify indicative expressions of them (e.g., indignation, dissatisfaction with job, joking relationships, disputes over payment, etc.) and to discover the conditions under which such expressions originate (e.g., status inconsistency, relative deprivation, frequency of supervision, etc.).[15] My concern here is not with these two questions, but with the nature of family and school experiences in which problems of equity and inequity are defined as such, and in which the underlying principles become established in children's minds.

Among children in a family, age is critical in determining what is fair and unfair.[16] In a sense, it is the clock by which we keep developmental time, changing constantly though not periodically. The gains and losses of life are inextricably tied to age; memory reminds us of what we once had, and the experiences of others inform us of our present standing and of what the future holds. The personal significance of age is heightened among young children because the younger they are, the more significant any given age difference between them. Thus the difference between a four-year old and an eight-year old is greater than that between a fourteen-year old and an eighteen-year old because, on the average, there are greater developmental changes occurring during the earlier four year span than during the later one. When the circumstances of life change rapidly; when one is still in the process of learning what is one's due and what is due others; and when the younger children do not have to fight the battles that the older ones have already won, it is difficult to determine whether one is being treated fairly on any given occasion.

In the family, except for the sense of unity and similarity that comes from experience in a small, solidary group whose members are reciprocally affectionate and supportive, behavior *within* the

CONTRIBUTION OF SCHOOLING TO THE LEARNING OF NORMS

setting is governed to a considerable extent by the unique personal characteristics of the members. Among children, as I have argued, age is one of the most important of these characteristics. Except in families with one child or multiple-birth children, age alone is sufficient to distinguish them, although it is certainly not the only distinguishing characteristic. Because of the developmental importance of age, it constitutes one basis according to which parents act toward their children and siblings act toward each other. There are, of course, occasions on which parents can and do treat their children as if they were alike, but where questions of responsibility, accountability, privilege, and the like are involved, the differences between children must be taken seriously. *In this sense,* and in the context of the earlier qualification about family unity, each child exists in his own set of circumstances and is treated accordingly. This statement does not deny that parents may in fact ignore the differences among their children. It does imply, though, that if they do so over the long run, there can be disruptive consequences for the children and for the family unit. As cases in point, there are well-known situations involving overdemandingness (treating children as if they were older), and overindulgence (treating them as if they were younger).

Questions of equity, always comparative, are tied to situations. As children grow older, their circumstances and those of siblings change. The basis on which they determine what is fair and unfair also changes both absolutely and relatively. Because age is a unique personal attribute, and because there are unique constellations of events and personal characteristics associated with small age spans, there are always variables at the root of equity problems. Inequities among young children can only be set straight in the relatively short run because circumstances in the short run change steadily over time.

The contrast between age as a constant and as a variable in questions of equity is evidenced clearly in Homans' treatment of age: *". . . one of the ways in which two men may be 'like' one another is in their investments [age being one]. Accordingly the more nearly one man is like another in age, the more apt he is to expect their net rewards to be equal and to display anger when his own are less."* [17] In the context of this statement, age is the criterion for assessing the fairness of rewards as one man compares his gain with that of another.

In the context of the transition between childhood and adulthood, two children *within the same family* (unless they are twins) cannot easily settle a question of equity by referring to their ages (they may acknowledge that the older child is entitled to more, but not how much more) because they differ in age, because the meaning of age differences changes, and because there can be disagreement over the coefficient for converting age units into units of gain and loss. Such a conversion is unnecessary in the case described by Homans because the two men are alike in age.

The problem families have of settling equity questions attributable to age variations does not arise in school classrooms, since the age of class members is nearly constant. Teachers cannot treat all pupils identically, but they can use age similarity as a guide for assigning similar instructional tasks to all members of a class and to communicate, implicitly or explicitly, that they are all in the same boat.

Even without age differences, problems of fairness and unfairness do arise in classrooms, originating when pupils who are supposed to be treated similarly are not so treated. Grades, for example, according to the usual procedure, must be assigned according to the quality of work completed, and equivalent products should receive the same grade. Marking similar work differently, or unequal work the same, represents unfair grading. A similar principle holds for the punishment of offenses (the punishment should fit the crime, and similar forms of misbehavior should be treated alike[18]) and for the assignment of tasks and responsibilities according to difficulty and onerousness. But there are secondary considerations that enter the process of evaluating performance: how hard pupils work and how much they have improved. These criteria cannot readily replace quality of performance unless teachers, pupils, and parents are willing to acknowledge the justice of various anomalies (so defined, at least, within the scope of American values), as when pupils who do excellent work with little effort receive lower grades than pupils who produce mediocre work through feverish activity; or when pupils who do not pull their weight in a cooperative project receive the high grade assigned to the project.

As argued earlier, equity involves a comparative assessment of one's circumstances: gains and losses, rewards and punishments, rights and obligations, privileges and responsibilities. To determine whether the circumstances in a given situation are equitable, an individual must learn to make comparisons by which he can discover whose circumstances resemble his own and whose do not, who is treated like him and who is not; he must also discover the relationships between his circumstances and the way he is treated.

Schooling, then, through the structural properties of classrooms at each school level and the treatment of pupils by teachers, provides opportunities for making the comparisons relevant to defining questions of equity far more effectively than does the family. The process is similar to that (above described) of learning the norm of universalism in general. Both within the classroom and within each grade, age (and, to a lesser extent, other personal and social characteristics) provides a basis for discovering both similarities and differences in categorical terms. The existence of grade levels distinguished primarily by the demandingness of work and demarcated by the device of yearly promotion, and the progression of pupils through them year by year, make it possible for children to learn that, *within the context of the school,* certain qualities that determine their uniqueness as persons become subordinated to those specific characteristics in which they are alike. Thus, fourth and fifth graders, despite their individuality, are judged according to the specific criterion of achievement, and the content and difficulty of their assigned tasks are regulated according to developmental considerations symbolized by grade. The fourth grader, having completed the third grade, can grasp the idea that he belongs to a category of persons whose circumstances differ from those of persons belonging to another category.

Family relationships are not organized on a group basis, nor do they entail anything comparable to the systematic step-by-step progression of grades in which the boundaries between one category and another are clearly demarcated. Although a child knows the difference between family members and nonmembers, his experiences in a kinship setting do not allow him to distinguish clearly whether his circumstances are uniquely his own or are shared. In other words, these relationships are not structured in such a way as to form a basis for making the categorical comparisons basic to the universalistic norm. Moreover, since parents treat their children in terms of the full range of personal characteristics; that is, according to the norm of diffuseness rather than that of specificity, the family setting is conducive to the special rather than the categorical treatment of each child (since the boundaries of a category are more clearly delineated if one characteristic, not many, constitutes the basis of categorization).

A CONCEPTUAL CAVEAT

The argument of this volume rests on the assumption that schools, through their structural arrangements and the behavior patterns of teachers, provide pupils with certain experiences largely unavailable in other social settings, and that these experiences, by virtue of their peculiar characteristics, represent conditions conducive to the acquisition of norms. I have indicated how pupils learn the norms of independence, achievement, universalism, and specificity as outcomes of the schooling process. A critical point, however, is how the relationship between experience and outcome is formulated.

There is no guarantee that pupils will come to accept these four norms simply because these experiences are available, nor should one conclude that these experiences contribute to the learning of only the four discussed here; for example, the pupils may lack the necessary social and psychological support from sources outside the school or sufficient inner resources to cope with the demands of schooling. These are reasons external to the school situation and may be sufficient to preclude both the instructional and normative outcomes. However, forces inherent in the schooling process itself may be equally preclusive, since the same activities and sanctions from which some pupils derive the gratification and enhancement of self-respect necessary for both kinds of outcome may create experiences that threaten the self-respect of others. Potentialities for success *and* failure are inherent in tasks performed according to achievement criteria. Independence manifests itself as competence and autonomy in some, but as a heavy burden of responsibility and inadequacy in others. Universalistic treatment represents fairness for some, cold impersonality to others. Specificity may be seen as situational relevance or personal neglect.

Within industrial societies where norms applicable to public life differ markedly from those governing conduct among kin, schools provide a sequence of experiences in which individuals, during the early stages of personality development, acquire new principles of conduct in addition to those already accepted during childhood. For reasons earlier enumerated in detail, the family, as a social setting with its characteristic social arrangements, lacks the resources and the competence[19] to effect the psychological transition. This is not to say that only the school can produce the necessary changes, but of those institutions having some claim over the lives of children and adolescents (e.g., the family, child labor, occupational apprenticeship, tutoring, the church, the mass media[20]), only the schools provide adequate, though not always effective, task experiences and sanctions, and arrangements for the generalization and specification of normative principles throughout many spheres of public life.

It is conceivable, of course, that families (and those other institutions as well as some yet to be invented) can provide the experiences necessary for the acquisition of these norms; family life provides opportunities for achievement, for assuming individual responsibility, and for categorical and specific treatment. Yet the family is more likely than schools to provide experiences that also undermine the acquisition of these norms. Similarly, the impact of the experiences that schooling provides may prove insufficient and inappropriate for their acquisition, and even if they are acquired, their acceptance is not necessarily of equal or great importance in all segments of public life. One thing that makes schooling effective is the relevance of the school's contribution to subsequent participation in public institutions. Another is the relationship between structural arrangements and activities in determining whether one setting or another is more conducive to producing a given outcome, for if two or more activities interfere with each other, or if the situation is inappropriate to the performance of an activity, the desired outcome is unlikely to appear.

AN IDEOLOGICAL CAVEAT

Although I have treated them as norms, independence and achievement have been regarded by many observers of the American scene as dominant cultural themes or values, general standards of what is desirable.[21] In view of this, it is important that the argument of this book not be taken as a defense of national values, although it should not surprise anyone that the normative commitments of individuals who have passed through American schools are generally (though not invariably) consistent with national values. The main purpose of this analysis is to present a formulation, hypothetical in nature, of how schooling contributes to the emergence of certain psychological outcomes, and not to provide an apology or justification for those outcomes on ideological grounds. I have avoided calling universalism and specificity cultural values even though both are norms, since few, if any, observers include them among the broad moral principles considered desirable in American life. Their exclusion from the list of values should further confirm the nonideological intent of this discussion.

Having the means to produce a desired result is not the same as an injunction to use them in producing it. Of the many considerations entering into the decision to employ available resources in creating even widely valued outcomes, the probable costs involved should give pause. For the norms in question here, whose desirability can be affirmed either on ideological grounds or in terms of their relevance to public life in an industrial society, conditions conducive to their development are also conducive to the creation of results widely regarded as undesirable. Thus, a sense of accomplishment and mastery, on the one hand, and a sense of incompetence and ineffectualness, on the other, both represent psychological consequences of continuously coping with tasks on an achievement basis. Similarly with independence: self-confidence and helplessness can each derive from a person's self-imposed obligation to work unaided and accept individual responsibility for his actions. Finally, willingness to acknowledge the rightness of categorical and specific treatment may indicate the capacity to adapt to a variety of social situations in which only a part of one's self is invested, or it may indicate a sense of personal alienation and isolation from human relationships.

From the viewpoint of ideological justification, the process of schooling is problematic in that outcomes morally desirable from one perspective are undesirable from another; and in the making of school policy the price to be paid must be a salient consideration in charting a course of action.

NOTES AND REFERENCES

1. William J. Goode, *World Revolution and Family Patterns,* p. 11, Free Press of Glencoe, New York (1963).

2. See, for example, Ruth Benedict, "Continuities and Discontinuities in Cultural Conditioning," in Clyde Kluckhohn, Henry

A. Murray, and David M. Schneider (eds.), *Personality*, pp. 522–531, Alfred A. Knopf, New York (1953); Talcott Parsons, "The School Class as a Social System: Some of its Functions in American Society," *Harvard Educational Review* **29**, No. 4, 297–318 (1959); and S. N. Eisenstadt, *From Generation to Generation*, pp. 115–185, Free Press, Glencoe, Ill. (1956).

3. S. N. Eisenstadt, *ibid.*, p. 164.

4. My emphasis here differs from Parsons' in that he views independence primarily as a personal resource: "... it may be said that the most important single predispositional factor with which the child enters the school is his level of *independence.*" Talcott Parsons, *op. cit.*, p. 300. Although independence is very likely such a predisposition—whether it is the most important single one is debatable—it is part of the school's agenda to further the development of independence to a point beyond the level at which family resources become inadequate to do so.

5. Winterbottom, for example, lumps independence and mastery together; the indices she uses to measure them, however, involve ostensibly different phenomena in that the mastery items refer to tendencies toward activity rather than to independence. Marian R. Winterbottom, "The Relation of Need for Achievement to Learning Experiences in Independence and Mastery," in John T. Atkinson (ed.), *Motives in Fantasy, Action, and Society*, pp. 453–478, Van Nostrand, Princeton (1958). As a definitional guideline for this discussion, I have followed the usage of Bernard C. Rosen and Roy D'Andrade, "The Psychosocial Origins of Achievement Motivation," *Sociometry* **22**, No. 3, 186 (1959) in their discussion of independence training; and of McClelland and his colleagues in a study of independence training, David C. McClelland, A. Rindlisbacher, and Richard DeCharms, "Religious and Other Sources of Parental Attitudes toward Independence Training," in David C. McClelland (ed.), *Studies in Motivation*, pp. 389–397, Appleton-Century-Crofts, New York (1955).

6. Kaspar D. Naegele, "Clergymen, Teachers, and Psychiatrists: A Study in Roles and Socialization," *Canadian Journal of Economics and Political Science* **22**, No. 1, 53 (1956).

7. See, for example, Marian R. Winterbottom, *ibid.*; Bernard C. Rosen and Roy D'Andrade, *op. cit.*, pp. 185–218; and Fred L. Strodtbeck, "Family Interaction, Values, and Achievement," in David C. McClelland *et al.*, *Talent and Society*, pp. 135–191, Van Nostrand, Princeton (1958).

8. For one attempt to treat athletics condescendingly as non-intellectualism, see James S. Coleman, *The Adolescent Society,* Free Press of Glencoe, New York (1961).

9. Rupert Wilkinson, *Gentlemanly Power,* p. 21, Oxford University Press, London (1964).

10. Although Parsons considers universalism-particularism to be a dichotomy, they are distinguished on at least two dimensions: cognitive and cathectic. "The primacy of cognitive values may be said to imply a *universalistic* standard, while that of appreciative values implies a *particularistic* standard. In the former case the standard is derived from the validity of a set of existential ideas, or the generality of a normative rule, in the latter from the particularity of the cathectic significance of an object or of the status of the object in a relational system." Talcott Parsons, *The Social System,* p. 62, Free Press, Glencoe, Ill. (1951).

11. Peter M. Blau, "Operationalizing a Conceptual Scheme: The Universalism-Particularism Pattern Variable," *American Sociological Review* **27,** No. 2, 169 (1962). The permission of Peter M. Blau to quote from his paper is gratefully acknowledged.

12. Peter M. Blau, *ibid.,* p. 164; my emphasis.

13. In the case of specificity, ". . . the burden of proof rests on him who would suggest that ego has obligations vis-à-vis the object in question which transcend this specificity of relevance." Talcott Parsons, *The Social System,* p. 65. In the case of diffuseness, ". . . the burden of proof is on the side of the exclusion of an interest or mode of orientation as outside the range of obligations defined by the role-expectation." Parsons, *ibid.,* p. 66.

14. For a discussion of relativity of perspective, see Daniel Lerner, *The Passing of Traditional Society,* pp. 43–75, Free Press of Glencoe, Glencoe, Ill. (1958). See also Chapter 6, below.

15. For discussions of these problems, see George C. Homans, *Social Behavior: Its Elementary Forms,* pp. 235–251, Harcourt, Brace, and World, New York (1961); Elliott Jaques, *The Measurement of Responsibility,* pp. 32–60, Harvard University Press, Cambridge (1956); and Leonard R. Sayles, *Behavior of Industrial Work Groups,* pp. 41–118, John Wiley and Sons, New York (1963). One proposition relating expressions about inequity and its conditions is the following: "The past occasions in which a man's activities have been rewarded are apt to have been occasions in which other men,

in some way like him, have been rewarded too. When others like him get their reward now, but he does not, he is apt to display emotional behavior." Homans, *ibid.*, pp. 73–74.

16. There are events in family life where the explanation that renders inequities fair lies not in age but in circumstances— "Your brother could stay home from school and watch television because he was sick (and you weren't)"—and in other personal characteristics beside age, such as sex—"It isn't safe for girls to walk home alone at that hour (but it's O. K. for your brother)."

17. George C. Homans, *ibid.*, p. 75.

18. Wheeler, in his investigation of Scandinavian prisons, cites the example of two men returned to prison following a joint escape; although they had committed the identical offense, one was judged to have escaped because of claustrophobic fears, the other because of persistent psychopathic tendencies. Their subsequent treatments differed according to medical criteria—open spaces for one, maximum security for the other—even though the separate treatments violated the dictum that the punishment should fit the crime; that is, same crime, same punishment. "Both among inmates who feel that their *sentences* are just and among those who feel they are unjust, the ones housed in preventive detention institutions [centers in which the nature of prison treatment is based in part on the personality characteristics of the offender] are less likely to have a sense of justice in the *treatment* they are receiving in the institution [than inmates held in custodial settings]." Stanton Wheeler, "Legal Justice and Mental Health in the Care and Treatment of Deviance," paper presented at the Meetings of the American Orthopsychiatric Association, San Francisco, April, 1966, p. 5.

19. For a discussion of competence as an organizational characteristic, see Philip Selznick, *Leadership in Administration,* pp. 38–56, Row, Peterson, Evanston, Ill. (1957).

20. Mary Engel, "Saturday's Children: A Study of Working Boys," Cambridge, Mass.; Harvard Graduate School of Education, Center for Research in Careers, Harvard Studies in Career Development No. 51, 1966; Carl I. Hovland, "Effects of the Mass Media of Communication," in Gardner Lindzey (ed.), *Handbook of Social Psychology, II,* pp. 1062–1103, Addison-Wesley, Reading, Mass. (1954); Blanche Geer *et al,* "Learning the Ropes: Situational Learning in Four Occupational Training Programs," in Irwin Deutscher and Elizabeth Thompson (eds.), *Among the People: Studies of the Urban Poor*, Basic Books, New York, in press.

21. For a general discussion of the concept of 'value' and of major American cultural themes, see Robin M. Williams, Jr., *American Society*, pp. 397–470, Alfred A. Knopf, New York (1960).

CHAPTER SIX

SCHOOLING AND CITIZENSHIP

[*Alfred Marshall*] *was taking as the standard of civilized life the conditions regarded by his generation as appropriate to a gentleman. We can go on to say that the claim of all to enjoy these conditions is a claim to be admitted to a share of the social heritage which in turn means a claim to be accepted as full members of the society, that is, as citizens.*

T. H. Marshall, "Citizenship and Social Class"

Traditional man has habitually regarded public matters as none of his business.

Daniel Lerner, *The Passing of Traditional Society*

The life of young children is bounded largely by relationships among kin and neighbors, but when they have grown to be adults, they participate in the institutional life of society as public persons outside the boundaries of the family. In industrial nations, formal schooling occupies much of the long transition between childhood and adulthood, so that to understand the contributions of schooling, one must determine its place in the network of other major institutions, especially the family, the economy, and the polity.

Some contemporary critics of the schools have come to question the relevance of schooling to subsequent adult life, and if one views the outcomes of schooling in the light of the rhetoric of educationists, the critics may not be too far from the mark. The question of relevance, as I view it here, boils down to this: *In what sense do the products of schooling contribute to the functioning of noneducational institutions?* And this question finds no answer in the ideological attacks and parries of schoolmen and their critics.

The contribution of schooling to the society at large and to specific institutions within it has been formulated in several ways. One of them treats schools as a means of distinguishing pupils according to psychological capacities more or less appropriate to later employment in occupations grouped according to broad social strata. Considerable emphasis is put on differences in academic achievement, the track system, and the separation of the college-bound from those destined to enter the job market either directly or shortly after leaving school. Parsons, for example, states:

In approaching the question of types of capacity differentiated . . . secondary school is the principal springboard from which lower-status persons will enter the labor force, whereas those achieving higher status will continue their formal education in college, and some of them beyond.[1]

A second formulation considers the school in terms of curricular objectives, primarily skills and subject matters whose relevance is usually judged in terms of its direct usefulness in later employment. This perspective on schooling usually manifests itself in efforts to reform the curriculum by providing vocational (industrial arts and trades), business, and commercial curricula for pupils not heading toward college, and developing the more exotic new curricula in mathematics, science, and social studies primarily for the college-bound. These latter curricula are more useful in jobs at the higher levels of the occupational hierarchy than for those obtainable directly after leaving high school, and for the "job" of getting through college; their vocational character should not escape attention even though the pejorative "vocational" is not usually applied to them.

A third sees schooling in terms of its contribution to rates of social mobility in the society at large; that is, in terms of the proportion of persons who have attended school for varying numbers of years who differ from their fathers in occupational attainment, and to the level at which they first entered the labor force.[2] All three formulations emphasize the connection between schooling and occupation. Important as this particular connection is, the nature of the relationship between schooling and nonoccupational (and nonfamilial) institutions has received less attention, though surely adult social participation involves more than employment.

I have taken the position that schooling represents a developmental process taking place outside of the family in which large masses of people acquire certain psychological capacities that enable them to participate in the major institutional areas of society, to occupy the component social positions of these areas, and to cope with demands and exploit the opportunities that these positions characteristically present. Within the almost limitless range of psychological capacities relevant to social participation, I am concerned only with the capacity to accept, and act according to, certain social norms: those of independence, achievement, universalism, and specificity. The number of major social institutions in society is much smaller, although still difficult to identify with any precision; yet I shall concern myself only with the polity and that segment of the economy consisting of occupational employment.

As described earlier, the acquisition of these four norms is related to the passage of pupils through a sequence of classroom experiences whose characteristics vary with school level and differ from those available within the family. By implication, the psychological capacities of people would be less well adapted to participation in the occupational and political realms of American society if their experiences were restricted largely to the household and its social environs. Similarly, occupational and political institutions would be less viable if they lacked the requisite human resources; specifically, large numbers of persons possessing capacities that enable them to cope with the requirements of participating in these institutions. That is to say, there must be some minimal "fit" between human characteristics and social demands if people are to participate in institutional life without undue psychological strain, and if the major institutions are to function adequately in getting the work of society done.

Earlier I suggested that one hypothetical answer to the question of what is learned in school is that pupils learn to accept certain social norms and to act according to them. But when schooling is viewed in the context of institutions other than the family, those that pupils are destined to enter following the completion of formal schooling, there is a different but complementary answer to the question: namely, psychological capacities, such as the four norms mentioned, that enable people to participate in and cope with the demands of modern occupational and political institutions, and to engage in the public life of society outside the household. This formulation emphasizes those outcomes of schooling that represent psychological resources "used" within the context of more than one social institution, not solely occupations, and differs from other formulations that consider outcomes conceived primarily in terms of the stated goals of the schools or in terms of their contribution to the extrusion of children from the conjugal family. My earlier attempt to contrast the structural properties of families and schools, along with the corresponding experiences that each setting provides, has importance not in its own right, but because the institutions of modern industrial societies make characteristic demands such that persons raised almost completely within conjugal or extended kinship units would be psychologically unprepared to cope with them. Some form of transitional mechanism, linking phases of the life cycle characterized by markedly different social demands, must then be available if large masses of people participating in the institutions of society shall be competent to meet those demands. Inkeles reminds us:

The main business of socialization is the training of infants, children, adolescents (and sometimes adults) so that they can ultimately fulfill the social obligations that their society and culture will place on them. Implicit in this statement is the expectation that, in meeting these societal demands, the individual will not be placed under so much strain as to fall apart psychologically.[3]

In earlier chapters I have described some of the structural properties of schools, contrasting them with those of the family, and indicating their relevance to the learning of certain norms. The task remains of describing some of the dominant properties of modern occupational and political institutions, particularly those of the United States with its highly industrialized economy and democratic polity, to whose operation the norms of independence, achievement, universalism, and specificity have particular relevance.

The United States, according to any defensible definition, is clearly a modern industrial nation; so too is the Soviet Union, even though both nations differ strikingly in political and economic organization. In fact, there are groups of characteristics common to the more industrially advanced nations, irrespective of widely recognized political, economic, and cultural differences, that distinguish them from the less advanced. For example, Harbison and Myers have indicated that industrially advanced nations have a higher per capita gross national product, a smaller proportion of the active population employed in agriculture, and a larger number of engineers and scientists per 10,000 population than those less advanced.[4] Most striking is the fact that the industrially advanced nations also invest most heavily in educational resources; they have more primary and secondary teachers per 10,000 population than the less advanced, more pupils enrolled in the particular primary and secondary school facilities characteristic of each nation, and more students enrolled in college.[5]

The Occupational System

One of the distinguishing characteristics of modern industrial nations is the existence of an occupational system in which the workplace is independent of the household and in which workers enter the economy through labor contracts or through self-employment in a comparatively free market:

Occupational roles, in the sense of specialized tasks within a division of labor, are nothing new in human history. . . . What is specifically modern is not specialization as such—although of course the development of modern technologies has been accompanied by a much greater degree of differentiation among occupational roles—but rather the very widespread separation of occupational roles from domestic life, and their location instead in specialized structures such as business firms and governmental bureaucracies.[6]

Some observers have argued that the growth of industrial systems has been accompanied by a decline of the extended family system and by an increase in the independence of individuals from large networks of kinsmen, but this is not necessarily the case.

In fact, emotional ties among the members of conjugal, mobile families are often intense, and there is substantial evidence that families provide both psychological and financial support for grown children in pursuit of an occupational career (sending them to college being one of the more important evidences of such support), and indicating that family ties may contribute to occupational attainment rather than detract from it by keeping young adults bound to the household.[7]

Being employed is perhaps the most important indication of adult status in industrial nations; being a husband, father, and voter simply do not suffice if a man is not also working at a job. Critics of the industrial order have attacked those parts of the occupational system appearing most inimical to man's free nature: the subordination of workers, repetitiveness of the work, minute scheduling of time and motion, and the narrow range of human talents actually involved in the performance of tasks. Marx and Engels leveled what is perhaps the most eloquent attack on the occupational order itself:

In communist society, where nobody has one exclusive sphere of activity but each can become accomplished in any branch he wishes, society regulates the general production and thus makes it possible for me to do one thing to-day and another to-morrow, to hunt in the morning, fish in the afternoon, rear cattle in the evening, criticize after dinner, just as I have a mind, without ever becoming hunter, fisherman, shepherd or critic.[8]

Whether or not one accepts the Marxian indictment, occupational employment does provide scope for individual expression, though probably more at the upper than at the lower levels of the hierarchy. It also determines the size of a person's income, hence the limits of his family's style of life and his social prestige, or standing, in the community. Alienating or not, work has a central place in the lives of industrial men:

The primordial meaning and function of work is dramatized by the narrow range of social contact of men squeezed out of the labor market; the aged, the school dropouts, the unemployed, and the underemployed are isolated from the mainstream of community life. Employment remains a symbol of one's place among the living.[9]

Given the importance of the occupational system in industrial societies and of employment in the personal lives of men, occupations tend to be ranked in much the same order in the most advanced nations. In a study of occupational prestige in the United States, Great Britian, the Soviet Union, Japan, New Zealand, and Germany, Inkeles and Rossi find:

> . . . an extremely high level of agreement [in rankings], going far beyond chance expectancy, as to the relative prestige of a wide range of specific occupations, despite the variety of socio-cultural settings in which they are found. This strongly suggests that there is a relatively invariable hierarchy of prestige associated with the industrial system, even when it is placed in the context of larger social systems which are otherwise differentiated in important respects.[10]

It may also suggest a broad similarity in the kinds of demands occupational tasks make on men and in the capacities men must possess in order to do their work.

The Middle Class

Important as employment is in the lives of industrial men, the ranking of occupations is perhaps the single most important criterion for establishing the hierarchy of social classes in industrial nations. Marx believed that as the capitalist-industrial system matured the middle class would become polarized with most of its members entering the proletariat (a minority entering the bourgeoisie) and then vanish prior to the advent of a revolution ushering in a new era in which occupations, along with the state, religion, and history, would cease to exist. History has not borne him out. The advance of industrialism has been accompanied not by the disappearance of the middle class but by its expansion and transformation, the burgeoning of the new middle class of professional, technical, service, and clerical workers, the emergence of new occupations at the same level, and the decline of the entrepreneurial old middle class so graphically chronicled by C. Wright Mills.[11] It can fairly be said that one distinguishing characteristic of modern industrial societies is the presence of a large middle class occupational sector. Hoselitz has noted the contrast:

> . . . one of the most characteristic aspects of a pre-industrial stratification system is the existence of a sharp polarity of social strata with an extremely steep pyramid of social ranking, a general gap between the

elite and the large masses, and a general disregard of economic per-
formance as an important status-conferring variable. . . . In the more
advanced countries . . . the middle class has attained a most important,
if not a decisive role. . . .[12]

The existence of a stratification system containing a large middle class means more than the availability of human resources capable of supporting a large industrial establishment; it constitutes a prime condition for the *political* stability of modern nations. Countries with large middle classes as well as skilled working classes whose members man the industrial, commercial, and professional establishments are relatively less susceptible to the effects of deep social cleavages than many Middle Eastern, Latin American, and Asian countries that are characterized by economic division into extremes of wealth and poverty and political division into controlling elite and subjugated mass. The relative absence of such cleavages is surely not sufficient to guarantee political stability (among modern industrial states, France and Germany have been plagued with unstable regimes) but sharp cleavage is indicative of highly divergent and polarized interests in a society making it difficult to achieve the allegiance of the populace to a unified political regime.

The Legitimate National Regime

The political stability of nations depends in part on the willingness of most of its members to acknowledge at least minimally the legitimacy of the regime, the *form* of government and the rules by which it operates: the means of attaining political office, the expression of opposition, the procedures for enacting and enforcing laws and settling disputes. (The concept of regime does not refer to the particular government or ruling group in power, which many members of the population, even a majority, may not support at any given time.[13]) Political stability is related to the operation of a government in that the performance of the government affects the needs and interests of the populace in very direct ways. It provides services, regulates the economy, declares war, adjudicates disputes, and protects its members, and to the extent that most of the people express at least minimal satisfaction with its performance, stability is lent to the regime:

Satisfaction with governmental output may lead an individual to sup-
port his political system, and high levels of such satisfaction are there-

*fore likely to foster political stability. For long-run stability, on the
other hand, a more diffuse sense of attachment . . . may be more significant.*[14]

But when societies are split by deep cleavages, acts of governments
affect people in such vastly different and conflicting ways as to
bring into relief the divergences in their interests.

The achievement of political stability, in the sense that a regime
has become legitimate within a given territory, usually represents
the outcome of historical processes in which critical political
problems have become solved. One such problem is succession
in office. Any political order must devise a viable method for
deciding who shall have the right to rule. A variety of solutions
have been worked out, ranging from the hereditary succession of
kings to the periodic popular election of presidents; all involve
some method of maintaining the loyalty of those segments of the
population opposed to the particular government in power, and
all involve acceptance of the methods for changing governments.
Solving the problem of succession, while crucial, does not suffice
to establish the stability of a political system, however. Disagreement over the right method by which one government shall follow
another may actually be a manifestation of other divisive social,
economic, or cultural interests, with the nature of the polity itself
hanging in the balance. These other cleavages must be closed or
at least mitigated before stability can be achieved.

Nations, of course, differ in their political histories, and the conflicts that have plagued one do not necessarily plague another.
Conflicts over religious, territorial, tribal, linguistic, racial, and
ethnic loyalties have posed threats to the stability of regimes in
more than one country. The problems engendered by these special
loyalties have come into prominence with the rapid emergence
of new states following the Second World War:

*A major problem in the civic integration of new states is the quicken-
ing of "primordial attachments" based on ties of blood, race, language,
region, religion or custom. These attachments give rise to separatist,
irredentist or factional groupings whose claims to recognition and
autonomy cut across the claims of civic unity based on a common
national territory.*[15]

All modern societies, even those most stable politically, contain
groupings whose interests and loyalties conflict sharply with each

other. In the United States, for example, cleavages based on social class became especially prominent during the Great Depression of the 1930's, religious differences between Catholics and Protestants have festered over the parochial school issue, and agitation over racial discrimination and the denial of full access to public facilities and services to Negroes has come to the forefront of political consciousness over the last fifteen years. Yet these divisions in the social order have been subordinated to a prior loyalty, held by masses of people, to an overarching civic order, to a national regime. This is not to deny that the fissures have been deep or that segments of the population have been sharply alienated; nor is it to deny that during the Civil War the nation came perilously close to splitting on a regional basis over the continuance and expansion of slavery.

The establishment of political unity in a nation depends on a balance of loyalties among its populace to the state as a whole and to subgroupings within it, and on the capacity of people to hold loyalties to more than one group at the same time:

[The] "longing not to belong to any other group" ... gives to the problem variously called tribalism, parochialism, communalism, and so on, a more ominous and deeply threatening quality than most of the other, also very serious and intractable problems the new states face....There are many other competing loyalties in the new states, as in any state—ties to class, party, business, union, profession, or whatever. But groups formed of such ties are virtually never considered as possible self-standing, maximal social units, as candidates for nationhood. Conflicts among them occur within a more or less fully accepted terminal community whose political integrity they do not, as a rule, put into question.[16]

When the members of some social grouping regard coexistence with competing groups as tantamount to joining with mortal enemies, political unity premised on allegiance to the commonweal becomes difficult or impossible to achieve. The nature of the state itself, the proper way to govern, and the appropriate means for settling disputes become critical issues. The conditions for social and political stability would not be met, according to Easton and Dennis, if "... each time a dispute arose [the regime] would have to seek to agree on means for settling differences at the same time as it sought to bring about a settlement of the substance of the issue."[17]

To the extent that primordial groups maintain their sentiments of exclusivity and social cleavages remain unresolved, there is little chance of developing a national polity in which major groups within the populace hold allegiance to the regime over the moderately long run.

The development of nations has been accompanied by the partial breakdown of autonomous, minority, sub-cultural groupings, which are based on tribe, religion, language, and the like, and of the primacy of loyalty to them. But such development has also been accompanied by an expansion in the people's interests from the parochial to those shared by broad segments of the population, and by an expansion in the scope of their social participation. In western nations, national development has been accompanied by: (1) shifts in economic life from agriculture to urban industrial and commercial pursuits, (2) change from dependence on the household of a feudal master to occupational employment, (3) extension of the rights of those who contribute economically to participate in the politics of the nation, and (4) replacement of church-controlled education, designed to maintain the interests of a particular corporate grouping, by state-controlled education that at the minimum provides literacy in a language spoken by most members of the nation.[18] In brief, national development has involved an extension of the rights and opportunities of persons to participate in the major nonfamilial institutions of society and to gain the capacities necessary to do so; that is, by the rise of citizenship.

Citizenship

The history of citizenship, according to T. H. Marshall, chronicles the extension of the rights mentioned above to all adult persons and the expansion of institutional areas open to participation. Marshall claims there are three parts to citizenship:

The civil element is composed of the rights necessary for individual freedom—liberty of the person, freedom of speech, thought and faith, the right to own property and to conclude valid contracts, and the right to justice. . . . By the political element I mean the right to participate in the exercise of political power, as a member of a body invested with political authority or as an elector of the members of such a body. . . . By the social element I mean the whole range from the right to a modicum of economic welfare and security to the right to share to the full in the social heritage and to live the life of a civilized being according to the standards prevailing in the society.*

The growth of national citizenship has involved primarily an extension of rights to people whose social position had previously prevented the holding of them, rights to express their interests and to participate in the affairs of the community at large, especially those of voting secretly and being represented at the seat of government. It represents, in other words, the advancement of civil, political, and social equality, together with corresponding changes in social arrangements and in the personal characteristics and actions of men. The extension of rights, moreover, was matched by obligations to accept governance according to rules having currency throughout the nation and to accept the enforcement of those rules by official agents of the state. The gradual equalization of social circumstances related to the extension of suffrage and representation was augmented by the opening of opportunities to enter into contracts, to form voluntary associations, and to receive a public education. These changes were accompanied by the decline of older forms of political involvement in which participation and representation were predicated on membership in the church, the nobility, and the guilds, and where masses of people could at best count on paternalistic forms of protection and support rather than political representation.

According to Bendix:

The French Revolution brought about a fundamental change in the conception of representation: the basic unit was no longer the household, the property, or the corporation, but the individual citizen; and representation was no longer channeled through separate functional bodies but through a unified national assembly of legislators.[19]

The emergence of the individual as the basic political unit did not, however, mean the disappearance of organized interests; men did not become social atoms before the state, alike in all respects. Given the right of voluntary association and the prevailing dif-

---

* From *Class, Citizenship, and Social Development,* by T. H. Marshall. Copyright © 1963 by T. H. Marshall. Reprinted by permission of Doubleday and Company, Inc.

ferences in religion, wealth, and occupation, each man could join
with others to express his interests in their variety.

It is characteristic of national political systems based on citizenship that a broad range of interests finds political expression
through representation, and that individual men possess several
social identities based on: (1) their location in society, (2) their
social characteristics, (3) their associations, (4) their interests,
and (5) the roles they play, not all of which are consistent; that is
to say, they have cross-cutting loyalties and seek to express the
interests based on them politically. Tocqueville, as is well known,
feared that with the continued development of an enfranchised
electorate, associations that mediated men's relationship to a
centralized state would decline, leaving men dangerously exposed
and vulnerable to the state even though they stood before it
equally. According to Rokkan:

*What Tocqueville was less ready to see was that this development
toward formal equalization could proceed pari passu with the steady
growth of a pluralistic network of associations and corporate bodies:
the systems of "one citizen, one vote" decision-making were gradually
balanced off, so to speak, against systems of bargaining, consultation
and representation among growing numbers of interest organizations,
voluntary associations and public bodies.*[20]

Tocqueville's apprehensions did materialize, however, in totalitarian states.

The Capacities of Citizens

These changes in the character of the polity and the concomitant
growth of industrial enterprise had important implications for the
political involvement of individuals. Occasions for contact with
civil authorities, the need to associate with others having both
similar and dissimilar interests, and the need to engage in the civic
affairs of the local community and the nation increased—in other
words, there were greater opportunities and a growing impetus
for participation in the community beyond the confines of the
family, the church, the ethnic enclave, and the household of
economically dominant landowners. The emergence of citizenship also brought about pressures for the development and diffusion of personal capacities hitherto restricted to elite groups;
skills for articulating one's interests verbally, fluency in a national

language, tolerance of diverse interests and viewpoints, and beliefs in one's own efficacy to influence events and conditions. Naturally, these changes did not occur equally in all countries, nor did all members of a particular country develop these capacities to the same extent. But in the western nations, particularly in those developing industrially, the trend was in this direction.

According to Lerner, there is a cluster of psychological capacities related to literacy that constitute prime conditions for the industrial and political development of nations and for the growth of citizenship within them: facility in the manipulation of symbols; the ability to imagine circumstances different from one's own, to put oneself in another person's position, and correlatively to compare one's own circumstances with those of others—in short, the capacity to empathize:

. . . high empathic capacity is the predominant personal style only in modern society, which is distinctively industrial, urban, literate and participant. *Traditional society is nonparticipant—it deploys people by kinship into communities isolated from each other and from a center; without an urban-rural division of labor, it develops few needs requiring economic interdependence; lacking the bonds of interdependence, people's horizons are limited by locale and their decisions involve only other* known *people in* known *situations. Hence, there is no need for a transpersonal common doctrine formulated in terms of shared secondary symbols—a national "ideology" which enables persons unknown to each other to engage in political controversy or achieve "consensus" by comparing their opinions.*[21]

The symbolic skills associated with literacy constitute a human resource of extraordinary ramifications. Literacy makes it possible for individuals to participate in the broad public domain of opinion and information far beyond the confines and events of the immediate locale; it is related, for example, not only to newspaper consumption, but also to radio listening and movie attendance, which do not depend on the ability to read but rather on the capacity to imagine and comprehend what is unfamiliar:

With literacy, people acquire more than the simple skill of reading. They gain access, in the very act of achieving distance and control over a formal language, to the world of vicarious experience and the complicated mechanism of empathy which is needed to cope with it.[22]

It thus represents a generalized symbolic medium enabling people to expand their horizons, become better informed, contemplate courses of action in the public arena, and understand their own circumstances in the wider context of current, past, and distant events. Literacy in a more immediate sense indicates command over the specific skills necessary to hold a job in an industrial or commercial enterprise and to participate in the political events of the day.

Schooling

Almond and Verba, in their comparative study of the United States, the United Kingdom, Germany, Italy, and Mexico describe the politically relevant capacities associated with schooling, and, according to Sutton:

The emergence of the modern state rested essentially on the universalization of citizenship and the corresponding attack on privileged statuses that this universalization implied. The demand that all men, however humble, be members of the state could not be separated from concern for their instruction.[23]

The more highly educated exceed the less well educated in awareness of the impact of government on individuals, command of political information, scope of political opinion, likelihood of engaging in political discussion, diversity of people with whom one carries on discussions, capacity to influence the government, extent of organizational memberships, and beliefs in the helpfulness and trustworthiness of others.[24] Stouffer, moreover, in his study of tolerance of nonconformity, shows that in all age groups of a national sample of the American population, the greater the number of years people have attended school, the more likely they will tolerate various forms of political nonconformity and ideological, racial, and cultural differences among people.[25]

Schooling and the associated advancement of literacy do not invariably form the basis of national unity and the development of citizenship; in societies in which only certain segments of the population distinguished by elite status, lineage, or religion have access to formal education either at home or abroad, the groundwork is laid for the perpetuation of social, economic, and political cleavages. Such societies divide into an educated elite and a relatively uneducated mass, or as in certain of the ex-colonial nations, those receiving western, liberal education readily become alienated from the masses whose schooling has been indigenous, inadequate, or nonexistent. Yet under different circumstances, most conspicuously when other conditions supporting the growth of industrialization and urbanization prevail, schooling will more likely contribute to the development of national unity than to the continuation of political cleavage.

SCHOOLING AND CITIZENSHIP

The idea of citizenship has two facets; it refers both to a set of institutional arrangements and to a set of human capacities. Citizens are persons who are psychologically competent to participate in the various social settings organized within public institutional areas because they possess the requisite human resources. Citizenship is a phenomenon characteristic of modern industrial societies, having developed along with the process of industrialization, but existing independently of the type of industrial economy and type of polity. Historically, the economic, political, religious, and educational functions have gradually been separated from units of kinship and have developed as independent institutional areas organized around their own characteristic set of activities and forms of social organization. The result has been the development of occupational specialties within each area, and the emergence of widespread public consumership oriented to each area. With respect to the economy, for example, Nash has said of primitive and peasant societies:

A family, a local group, a compound of patrons and clients may be a producing unit, but its productive activities are but one of the areas meeting the maintenance needs of the group. Conflicts and choices over the use of time and resources in these productive units will be resolved and made with reference to the total calculus of the many purposes of the group rather than by the single magnitude of output or economic return.[26]

The same might be said of political, religious, and educational activities in these societies, respectively for each area.

The emergence of institutions distinct from the family has been accompanied by other secular changes; parochial ties based on region, religion, lineage, language, race, and ethnicity have weakened, and there has been a corresponding increase in the opportunities for social contact among persons of diverse background and interests. There has also been a gradual and widespread acquisition of certain personal capacities, most conspicuously literacy and facility in the manipulation of symbols (language and money being among the most important), tolerance of social differences, an extension of the range of persons with whom one can establish relationships of trust, and a sense of individual efficacy in contributing to the commonwealth.

What the development of citizenship is in the history of industrialism and of nation states, schooling is in the life-histories of industrial men, in that it produces changes in the state of mind that enable men to participate in a public life outside the circle of the family. The beginning of school at age six signals the first major departure from a setting in which the main participants are related through particularistic ties and whose interests in each other are predominantly diffuse. The central activities involved in the experience of schooling are judged primarily according to achievement standards, the same standards that will later apply in the world of work. The standards apply to everybody in all age groups required by the state to attend school; school attendance, in other words, is obligatory. At varying time intervals after the minimum legal age for leaving school, access to public facilities and rights of participation become available, *at least in principle,* to all members of the state: to hold a job, to enter into contracts, to vote, to hold public office, to use public transportation, to sue, to own property, to benefit from provisions for public welfare. Legitimate exceptions are usually governed according to age (as is the case with voting, holding certain public offices, and receiving social security), and according to extraordinary extenuating circumstances (such as loss of civil rights upon being incarcerated, criteria that themselves apply categorically). There are, of course, illegitimate exceptions, such as racial, religious, and ethnic discrimination, but the fact that these phenomena prove to be sources of national embarrassment indicates the universalistic nature of the principle of public access and participation.

A basic element of citizenship is the principle of equality, a representation of the similarities among people; in whatever respect people are like each other, and where that likeness distinguishes them from others, they constitute a category. The larger the category, whether it be based on personal characteristics or circumstances, the greater the number of individual differences that must be ignored in classifying people within it; thus, for example, to speak of the brotherhood of man is to state a moral principle that subordinates all differences between men to the common bond among them. Citizenship, less broadly, refers to the bases of unity among men in a nation rather than throughout mankind. But if equality is the basis of citizenship, then diversity is the basis of family life. Within units of kinship, however unified, it is the differences among members (particularly those of age, sex, and generation) rather than the similarities that become the main reference points for members' conduct toward each other. If the premises of conduct governing family life are generalized beyond the confines of kinship units (as indeed they are in many societies), one would not expect to find citizenship as one of the main organizing principles of society. Societies, instead, would be organized in groupings that in one respect or another made claims for special status.

The development of large industrial nations has to a large extent determined the particular bases on which the members of society shall be considered equals (that is, the criteria of citizenship) and correspondingly, the criteria that no longer disqualify people from becoming citizens. The developments that T. H. Marshall has traced historically continue in the contemporary United States with the *de jure* extension of the franchise to women (1920), its *de facto* extension to Negroes (who have had the franchise *de jure* since 1870), and most currently with the proposed extension to juvenile offenders of the right to counsel. In the latter case, the principle of citizenship gives primacy to the equality that unites offenders: that they should be granted rights that supersede the prior distinction between children and adults. That is, a new similarity takes precedence over an old difference, just as equality before the sovereign took precedence over property qualifications, prior conditions of servitude, and the like. But if familism and citizenship are so divergent in principle, some social mechanism must be available for individuals to learn each principle and the circumstances under which it applies. One such mechanism, and the dominant one in industrial societies, is the school, for the school, through the process of sequential categorization that I have described earlier, provides settings in which individuals form an increasing number of new equalities, and thereby provides situations in which they can learn how to subordinate differences to similarities, both specifically and generally. It is the acquired capacity to do this that constitutes one of the prime bases of citizenship.

Thus far, I have spoken of the characteristics of modern nations as if all were of a piece. Despite evident similarities, such as their large industrial establishments and their hierarchies of occupational prestige, the United States, Germany, France, and the Soviet Union, for example, differ conspicuously from each other politically as well as in the nature of their industrial economic systems. But my interest in schooling here extends primarily to the American case, which is that of an advanced industrial nation with a stable, two-party, democratic political system. In the following chapter, I shall be concerned with showing how the normative outcomes of American schooling contribute to the widespread acquisition of capacities that support an industrial occupational system, a two-party democratic political system, and the integration of family units with the public spheres of occupation and politics.

NOTES AND REFERENCES

1. Talcott Parsons, "The School Class as a Social System: Some of its Functions in American Society," *Harvard Educational Review* **29**, No. 4, 313 (1959).

2. See, for example, Joseph A. Kahl, *The American Class Structure*, pp. 276–298, Rinehart, New York (1957); and C. Arnold Anderson, "A Skeptical Note on the Relation of Vertical Mobility to Education," *American Journal of Sociology* **66**, No. 6, 560–570 (1961).

3. Alex Inkeles, "Social Structure and the Socialization of Competence," *Harvard Educational Review* **36**, No. 3, 279 (1966). Inkeles, rightly, does not limit his discussion of socialization to the development of only those capacities directly relevant to meeting externally-imposed social demands; he includes as well capacities related to the achievement of purely personal aspirations.

4. Frederick Harbison and Charles A. Myers, *Education, Manpower, and Economic Growth*, p. 39, McGraw-Hill, New York (1964).

5.   Frederick Harbison and Charles A. Myers, *ibid.*, p. 38. Harbison and Myers include the following in their list of most advanced nations, in ascending order of development: Denmark, Sweden, Argentina, Israel, West Germany, Finland, Soviet Union, Canada, France, Japan, United Kingdom, Belgium, Netherlands, Australia, New Zealand, United States. *Ibid.*, p. 48.

6.   Lloyd Fallers, "Equality, Modernity, and Democracy in the New States," in Clifford Geertz (ed.), *Old Societies and New States,* p. 181, Free Press of Glencoe, New York (1963).

7.   See William J. Goode, *World Revolution and Family Patterns,* pp. 70–76, Free Press of Glencoe, New York (1963), and Eugene Litwak, "Occupational Mobility and Extended Family Cohesion," *American Sociological Review* 25, No. 1, 9–21 (1960).

8.   Karl Marx and Friedrich Engels, *The German Ideology,* p. 22, International Publishers, New York (1939).

9.   Harold L. Wilensky, "Varieties of Work Experience," in Henry Borow, (ed.), *Man in a World of Work,* p. 148, Houghton Mifflin, Boston (1964). The permission of Harold L. Wilensky to quote from his paper is gratefully acknowledged.

10.   Alex Inkeles and Peter H. Rossi, "National Comparisons of Occupational Prestige," *American Journal of Sociology* 61, No. 4, 339 (1956).

11.   C. Wright Mills, *White Collar,* Oxford University Press, New York (1951), *passim,* but especially pp. 63–76.

12.   Bert F. Hoselitz, "Social Stratification and Economic Development," *International Social Science Journal* 16, No. 2, 247 (1964).

13.   For a more complete discussion of the concepts of regime and government and the distinction between them, see David Easton, "An Approach to the Analysis of Political Systems," *World Politics* 9, No. 3, 383–400 (1957); and David Easton and Robert D. Hess, "Youth and the Political System," in Seymour Martin Lipset and Leo Lowenthal (eds.), *Culture and Social Character,* pp. 226–251, Free Press of Glencoe, New York (1961).

14.   Gabriel A. Almond and Sidney Verba, *The Civic Culture,* p. 242, Princeton University Press, Princeton (1963).

15.   Charles E. Woodhouse and Henry J. Tobias, "Primordial Ties and Political Process in Pre-Revolutionary Russia: The Case

of the Jewish Bund," *Comparative Studies in Society and History* **8,** No. 3, 331 (1966).

16. Clifford Geertz, "The Integrative Revolution," in Geertz (ed.), *Old Societies and New States,* p. 111.

17. David Easton and Jack Dennis, "The Child's Acquisition of Regime Norms: Political Efficacy," *American Political Science Review* **61,** No. 1, 25 (1967).

18. For a general discussion of these trends, see Reinhard Bendix, *Nation-Building and Citizenship,* pp. 55–104, John Wiley and Sons, New York (1964).

19. Reinhard Bendix, *op. cit.,* p. 94.

20. Stein Rokkan, "Mass Suffrage, Secret Voting and Political Participation," in Lewis A. Coser (ed.), *Political Sociology,* p. 107, Harper and Row, N.Y. (1966).

21. Daniel Lerner, *The Passing of Traditional Society,* p. 50, Free Press of Glencoe, New York (1958).

22. Daniel Lerner, "Communications Systems and Social Systems: A Statistical Exploration in History and Policy," *Behavioral Science* **2,** No. 4, 272 (1957).

23. Francis X. Sutton, "Education and the Making of Modern Nations," in James S. Coleman (ed.), *Education and Political Development,* p. 57, Princeton University Press, Princeton (1965).

24. Gabriel A. Almond and Sidney Verba, *The Civic Culture,* pp. 317–318.

25. Samuel A. Stouffer, *Communism, Conformity, and Civil Liberties,* pp. 89–108, Doubleday, Garden City (1955). Among other types of "nonconformity," Stouffer includes: allowing a Communist to make a speech in one's community, not removing a book written by a Communist from the public library, not firing a Communist radio singer, etc.

26. Manning Nash, *Primitive and Peasant Economic Systems,* p. 24, Chandler, San Francisco (1966).

CHAPTER SEVEN

SCHOOLING, WORK,
AND POLITICS

Universalistic religions making oaths to strangers sacred, universalistic law making contracts between strangers binding, reliable negotiable instruments so that one can trust the paper and not the man, ethics of achievement according to impersonal standards in occupational life, rather than interpenetration of occupational and kinship life, all clearly make it easier to construct social systems out of groups of strangers.

Arthur L. Stinchcombe, "Social Structure and Organizations"

In the democratic mind, "special privilege" is the worst of political crimes.

Louis Hartz, "Democracy: Image and Reality"

The work of a modern industrial society, in its major institutional areas, is carried on by persons who are located in specialized social positions. According to Shils:

A rational economic system requires enterprisers and managers, economists, accountants, chemists, agronomists, lawyers, and experts in transportation and marketing. Public political life requires politi-

cians, party officials, editors and reporters, professors and social re-
search workers, radio engineers and producers. These professions can
neither be staffed nor carried on without a modern intellectual system.[1]

And of course, one could reasonably add educational and religious
roles to the economic and political ones included in Shils' statement.
People do not participate directly in the economy or in the polity,
two of the broad institutional areas of society; they hold jobs and
engage in political activities. As jobholders, they agree to accept
certain obligations: to complete a given amount of work in a given
amount of time, to associate with other persons in specified
ways, and to submit themselves and the things they produce to
the review of others. The element of externally imposed demand is
clearly evident. Yet work is not all demand; depending on the job,
there are opportunities for free expression, for planning over the
long run, for choosing freely among real options, and for putting
one's personal stamp on what one does. In politics, except for
persons holding elective or appointive office, the elements of
demand are far less conspicuous. There is the right to vote, and
there are opportunities to participate in a variety of ways in
political campaigns. No compulsion is involved; there are no formal or contractual obligations to meet.

With jobs, it is often easy to see the connection between demands
and opportunities, on the one hand, and the personal capacities
of the jobholder, on the other. Laboring jobs, for example, require
a certain amount of physical strength; a weak man simply cannot
meet the demands of the work. Other jobs, particularly professional ones, require a certain detachment from the personal concerns of clients; practitioners who become too deeply involved
cannot provide the professional service effectively. In the political
realm, the aspect of demand is more subtle, but still present.
Consider the following:

How could a mass democracy work if all the people were deeply in-
volved in politics? Lack of interest by some people is not without
its benefits, too. True, the highly interested voters vote more, and
know more about the campaign, and read and listen more, and partic-
ipate more; however, they are also less open to persuasion and less
likely to change. Extreme interest goes with extreme partisanship and
might culminate in rigid fanaticism that could destroy democratic
processes if generalized throughout the community.[2]

Implied here is the proposition that a working democracy contains within it an electorate composed of people who possess a range of personal capacities: some who are deeply concerned, active, and opinionated; others who are less interested, less informed, less fired up. And if the balance of capacities shifts too far in either direction, conditions favoring the continued operation of the polity, such as the need for compromise and give-and-take on specific issues, may not be adequately met.

An industrial occupational system and a political democracy both depend on the availability of large masses of people who possess personal capacities appropriate to the demands of social positions and to the performance of required activities. It is premature to speak of necessary or sufficient conditions. Schools are not the only social agency that generates these institution-supporting capacities, but they are certainly a critical one. It remains to show how their normative products contribute to the support of these other institutions.

THE OCCUPATIONAL WORLD

It is one thing to speak of the place of occupations in industrial nations, and another to describe the character of work at points where it touches the lives of people. Kerr and his colleagues describe the work force:

> [Men] dedicated to hard work, a high pace of work, and a keen sense of individual responsibility for performance of assigned norms and tasks. . . . Industrialization requires an ideology and an ethic which motivate individual workers. Strict supervision imposed on a lethargic work force will not suffice; personal responsibility for performance must be implanted within workers, front-line supervisors, and top managers.[3]

Beyond this very general description, the American labor force—indeed, any industrial labor force—is characterized by (1) the separation of the workplace from the household, (2) a distinction between the worker as a person and the position he occupies, (3) widespread employment in large-scale organizations with both bureaucratic and professional forms of authority, (4) individual accountability for the performance of tasks judged according to standards of competence, and (5) by the affiliation of individuals to organizations through *ad hoc* contractual agreements. The division of labor characteristic of nonindustrial societies differs markedly in contrast:

The division of labor [in primitive and peasant societies] is not extensive; neither is it socially organized in a manner requiring clear specification of direct producer, supervisor, and policy-maker which underlie the bureaucratic structure of a modern intensive and extensive division of labor. . . . An occupational list in a peasant or primitive society is not a long one, and the interdependence between jobs and tasks tends to be chronological and sequential, rather than synchronous or simultaneous as in industrial economies. . . . With the small differences in skill in productivity, work and tasks are apportioned to the appropriate persons without much regard for effects on output.[4]

Separation of Workplace and Household

According to Parsons: *"Max Weber, perhaps more than any other social scientist, has emphasized the importance of the structural differentiation between the household and the organization in which members of the household perform occupational roles."*[5] This process has occurred along with the urbanization of the economy and the related decline of an agricultural economy composed of families farming for their own consumption, and the growth of occupational pursuits dependent on the availability of capital equipment beyond the financial resources of families. Yet even when the "means of production" fall within the jurisdiction of the household, the separation of job and home still occurs, if only taking the symbolic yet real form of using part of the home as an "office" (and duly taking a tax deduction for the expense of running it).

Certain forms of agriculture, industry, and commerce can be run within a family context, but with the advent of large industrial establishments the family has declined as a viable unit of economic production. Occupational pursuits are carried on within large organizational settings explicitly designed for the accomplishment of specific goals: the manufacture of products, the provision of services, the advancement of knowledge, the extraction of substances from the earth. The involvement of people in these activities must to a large extent be governed by calculations that link means to ends rationally and economically in the service of the specific goals of the productive process itself and of maintaining the organization in which productive energies and resources are brought together. This means in most cases the subordination of personal attachments, of relationships of emotional solidarity—typical of family life and friendship—to the demands of production and of those occupational endeavors designed to further it. As a result, the obligations of work and family are usually insulated and separated from each other.

The physical and symbolic separation of household and workplace is related to the more general distinction between private and public interest. Private interests pertain primarily to the family and are governed largely by ties of affection, solidarity, mutual support, and personal loyalty, the welfare of the solidary family unit and its members being the prime consideration. Public interests pertain more to the welfare of the community at large than to that of particular families within it, and rules of conduct designed to serve the public interest must apply to all. Public welfare—and I do not limit the term "public" to governmental—and community interest are usually defined in terms of classes of people and classes of situations: children between given ages must attend school, passengers on conveyances pay the same fees for rides of the same distance, persons committing offenses receive punishments related to the nature of the offense, and so on through the gamut of situations in which persons participate in the public sector as members of occupations and as clients of others in *their* occupational capacities.

Particularly at those points where the realms of occupation and politics converge, that is, among elected and appointed officials of government, the law usually delineates the boundary between public and private interests by means of the so-called conflict-of-interest laws:

The most obvious of all conflict-of-interest principles is that a public employee does not act in his official capacity with respect to matters in which he has a private stake. . . . [Law] prohibits a state employee from knowingly participating in a particular matter in which he or persons to which he is related through family or business had a financial interest.[6]

This type of conflict clearly does not arise when the family is the fundamental economic and political unit.

Distinction between the Worker and His Position

The second characteristic of the labor force is based on the distinction between the worker as a person and the job he holds. This same distinction also appears in the political arena where men are elected to "office" and where the office exists both before and after the term of any one occupant. The independence of man and office becomes most conspicuous, for example, following the death of a president; the vice president succeeds to the Presidency and the Vice Presidency continues to exist, even though unoccupied until the next election. In the more mundane world of everyday affairs, the familiar sign, "Help Wanted," appearing in store windows or in the classified ad columns of newspapers, speaks a message more complex than is usually recognized. It means, aside from the obvious fact that someone is needed to work, that there is an empty position to be filled. A position has no tangible reality, but its "existence" becomes evident when it is unoccupied, when the creation of jobs is followed by a search for men to do them, and when crises over succession to office arise. The case of succession is particularly interesting when a person with charismatic qualities must be replaced, for it becomes immediately apparent that the person cannot be replaced, that in fact he occupied a unique position all along, whether or not he was recognized as doing so, and that this position remains to be "filled" even though the activities associated with it may already be performed by another person.[7]

The idea that positions refer at the minimum to clusters of activities and that these clusters can be changed or eliminated is highly characteristic of industrial occupations in organizational settings, although certainly not peculiar to them. Barnard, for example, clearly distinguished between personal membership in an organization and the member's contribution of effort expended in the interest of the organization. *"When we say,"* he states, *"that we are concerned with a system of coordinated human efforts, we mean that although persons are agents of the action, the action is not personal in the aspect important for the study of cooperative systems."*[8] That is, an individual whose affiliation with the organization is one of occupational employment is expected to invest only parts of his person and his energy in organizational interests; those parts, in other words, related to selling insurance, driving a truck, writing columns for a newspaper, or whatever the line of work happens to be, and getting along with clients, colleagues, and bosses as the job requires. In the nature of the case, individuals actually put more of themselves into their jobs than the organizationally defined and expected contribution, and this fact is recognized within the organization by the kinds of incentives held out to men, as Barnard was well aware:

The contributions of personal efforts which constitute the energies of organizations are yielded by individuals because of incentives. The egotistical motives of self-preservation and of self-satisfaction are dominating forces; on the whole, organizations can exist only when consistent with the satisfaction of these motives. . . . The individual is always the basic factor in organization.[9]

And although self-satisfaction and self-preservation by no means exhaust the motives that individuals bring to organizations, the point is that incentives must be sufficient to attract persons, not simply to attract their contributions.

Bureaucratic and Professional Authority

The distinction between the person and the position is central to the third characteristic of an industrial labor force: employment in large-scale organizations. According to the U.S. Census, in 1964 about 85% of American nonagricultural workers 14 years of age or older were employed in governmental and other nonhousehold capacities for wages and salaries; the self-employed represented slightly under 10% of the work force.[10] Although these figures do not provide detailed description of the characteristics of employing organizations or of the extent to which they are bureaucratized (other than the fact that they are larger than households), they clearly indicate that organizational affiliation in employment is extremely widespread. One of the most important characteristics of employment in large-scale organizations is the prevalence of authority relationships based on both bureaucratic and professional principles.

The division of labor within organizations can be described from many different perspectives, but one of the major considerations is the distinction between those who perform the central work activities (e.g., working on an assembly line, treating persons who are sick, selling groceries, teaching children, etc.) and those who perform managerial functions (e.g., obtaining necessary resources from the external environment and allocating them internally, setting standards of work performance, establishing relationships with other organizations, etc.), functions related to committing the resources of the whole organization or of substantial segments of it.[11]

Persons occupying managerial positions are usually involved in relationships of authority with subordinates according to bureaucratic principles that depend on the nature of the organization; that is, subordinates follow directives because they originate from a person in a superordinate position who is authorized to give them, because the content of the directives falls within a previously agreed-upon range of concerns, and because both subordinate and superordinate acknowledge the legitimacy of rules that justify the superordinate's right to give the directive. That is to say, bureaucratic authority links the members of an organization, considered as belonging to classes of order-givers and order-receivers, through a specific range of concerns. This type of authority is based primarily on the incumbency of a position rather than on technical expertise or electoral support, and is most characteristically found in certain branches of the military and civil service, and in the lower and middle levels of both commercial and industrial enterprises, all of which depend to a considerable extent on large numbers of technical and production workers performing fairly routine and repetitive activities.

Authority based on professional expertise is far from unknown in such organizations and usually takes the form of persons working at the managerial level in staff (advisory) capacities. It is not the hierarchical position of staff members that lends authority to their directives, but rather their specialized, technical knowledge specifically related to the manager's area of responsibilities. The staff member's subordinates are not those who occupy a lower position hierarchically; rather, they are persons at roughly the same level who are less knowledgeable, less competent in certain technical areas.

Organizations do not engage professional persons and experts solely in staff capacities; in fact, certain organizations, such as hospitals, schools, law firms, universities, research institutes, and the like, are expressly built to provide professional services for clients and to create original knowledge. In such cases, professionals are themselves the technical workers; they are not advisors to managers who direct workers performing relatively routine tasks. Organizations of this type usually have dual systems of authority: one governing relations between professionals and clients, with due regard for loyalty to the client's interests and for the professional's free exercise of expert judgment; the other governing relations between the managerial and professional components, with due regard for the collegial interests of practitioners and for standards of practice originating in the wider community of professionals rather than in the administrative hierarchy of the organization. Professional authority is primarily oriented to the solution of specific classes of problems through the application of expert knowledge: to the design and construction of buildings, the curing of illnesses, the saving of souls, the litigation of legal disputes.

Even though bureaucratic and professional organizations differ structurally, their authority relations are based on the same principles. The conduct of superiors toward subordinates in bureaucratic settings is often governed by general principles which apply to *types* of cases and exigencies: rules and regulations pertaining to safety, the filling out of forms, times of arrival and departure, preferred channels of communication, particular classes of individuals, and the like. Similarly with professionals and their clients, conduct is to a considerable extent derived from scientific knowledge, legal precedent, or theological principle, and is applied to types of illness, offenses, or moral predicaments brought to the practitioner by a particular person.

In both cases, relationships of authority center around characteristics abstracted from the whole man. Thus, in an industrial setting, the conduct of a supervisor will be governed largely by the fact that his subordinates are linked to him in several ways: through the terms of a contract setting out and drawing boundaries around mutual rights and obligations, by jurisdictional boundaries limiting the activities that a worker can legally perform, by rules of seniority; in short, by a set of considerations applying not to individuals *per se*, but to classes of them falling within a category based on some specific characteristic. This is not to suggest that personal and other considerations form no part of authority relations in industrial settings; quite the contrary. It is simply to contend that categorical bases of conduct have a prominent place, and that individuals who cannot form associations with others on this basis may well have a difficult time of it as employees.

In a professional relationship, such as that obtaining between a doctor and his patient, the conduct of each is governed not so much by organizational rules and regulations as by the physician's command of general medical principles applied to *types* of illness. Whatever the extent of his personal concern with the individual patient—and with many physicians this is considerable—he cannot express this concern to an extent that it compromises a technically defensible treatment of the illness. In hospitals, in contrast to private offices, rules do regulate certain aspects of doctors' conduct, but they pertain more to the smooth operation of the hospital than to techniques of patient care. The actual treatment of disease in hospital settings follows the same general medical principles that apply in private practice.

The contrast between modern medicine and other medical traditions is dramatic indeed, as evidenced by the following description of medical care among Spanish-Americans:

In time of sickness one expects his family to surround and support him, and to supervise closely and critically, if not actually carry on, the treatment process. Members of the family, in turn, feel obligated to remain close to the patient, to take charge of his treatment, to reassure him as to his place in and importance to the family group.[12]

Clearly, medical treatment in this cultural group consists more in maintaining family solidarity and securing the place of the individual within the kinship unit than in applying an esoteric technology based on general scientific and therapeutic principles to the causes and symptoms of disease. Not surprisingly, there has been great concern within the medical profession over the frequent failure to treat the whole person, a concern that has prompted reforms in the training of physicians: extending clinical training back into the first and second years of medical school and giving medical students responsibility for the medical care of whole families. These changes, however, have not stemmed the tide of medical specialization and referral.

Authority relations in both bureaucratic and professional settings center around a circumscribed and often stipulated set of interests shared by superior and subordinate, and by practitioner and client.

In the bureaucratic setting, employment contracts set forth the rights and obligations of both parties. If superiors give orders that exceed the provisions of the contract, subordinates can refuse to obey them without being insubordinate; by the same token, superiors can refuse to provide extra services and rewards. This is not to suggest that the terms of an employment contract are the sole determinants of the relationship between superiors and subordinates; far from it. The literature on industrial and bureaucratic organizations abounds with examples of informal conduct ranging outside the terms of contract.[13] The point is, however, that employment contracts are primarily designed to attach individuals to organizations in a way that will maximize their contribution to the technical imperatives of the production process; assuming the adequacy of their motivation to work and their satisfaction with the workplace and with the inducements held out for them, workers are hired largely—though not solely—according to the degree and appropriateness of specific skills to the demands of the job.[14]

In the professional setting, to continue the medical example, the scope of a practitioner's interest in his clients manifests itself in the old and difficult dilemma of whether to treat the patient or his illness. The two alternatives are by no means mutually exclusive, and the balance between them varies with the medical specialty with neither alternative ever really disappearing. Given the nature of modern medical technology and training, physicians are constrained to narrow their interests to the nature of the disease and its cure, justifying inquiries beyond this range of concerns in terms of their relevance to diagnosis and treatment. Moreover, the growth of medical specialization and referral has fostered a decline in the scope of a doctor's interest in his patients as people. At least in the large cities, the days of the general practitioner appear numbered; he is being replaced in good measure by the clinic with its waiting lines and brief visits with an "attending" rather than a "family" physician, and by the specialist who is called in when particular symptoms appear and who vanishes when they vanish. Even the psychiatrist, whose license to inquire is perhaps widest of all the specialists and whose contacts with patients are prolonged, may actually learn about only a narrow segment of the patient's life because of doctrinal limitations on what questions are important and the limits imposed by the office setting on the scope of his observations of conduct related to mental illness.

As in the case of industrial and other bureaucratic settings, authority relations between professionals and clients are based primarily on considerations relevant to the effective performance of a task; effective, that is, within limits determined by the available technology. Effective performance of a task means coping with those specific problems that fall within one's area of expertness, no matter what the characteristics of the person presenting them. In the case of medical practice, there is evidence that reveals a connection between technical competence and holding preferences, contrary to medical ethics, for particular types of patients. Martin, in a study of fourth-year medical students, shows that the greater a student's confidence in his ability to perform specific medical procedures, the fewer the preferences, unrelated to disease, he holds for particular types of patients.[15] The formal contractual component of professional authority relations is less prominent; a fee is set in exchange for a commitment of best effort and best judgment but without a promise of successful outcome. (Compare this to a manufacturer's guarantee to deliver goods or services in a given quantity, by a certain date, and in good condition.) Yet the professional does guarantee his service will be relevant to the problems presented by his clients. Adherence to these standards is usually governed by the practitioner's past training, by the ethical strictures of his profession, and by the reactions of his client when his conduct borders on exploitation or the invasion of privacy, rather than by formal, organizational rules.

Accountability and Competence

The fourth characteristic of an industrial labor force is that job performance is judged according to criteria of competence and of individual accountability. In most lines of work, it matters how well a person does his job. For many jobs this is true because occupational activities contribute to some larger product whose completion depends on the successful accomplishment of prior tasks; in others, the quality of outcome is important because a product or service is consumed directly and the satisfaction of the consumer rests in the balance. These are external constraints generating concern with competent performance; other constraints are internal to the individual: a sense of self-discipline, of crafts-manship, of concern with standards of excellence, of mastery. But in most all occupational pursuits, employment itself, remuneration, and promotion are more closely tied to the quality of past and present performance (and to the promise of future performance), than to personal attributes, family ties, or social characteristics. The high priority placed on performance standards is supported by the existence of a cadre of specialized workers having supervisory responsibilities and by an elaborate social machinery: training institutions for the acquisition of appropriate skills, licensing procedures that certify minimum credentials, civil service regulations for promotion, formal testing procedures to measure proficiency, and in-service training.

Most occupations, and particularly those carried on within organizations, are so organized that individual contributions to the completion of isolated, collective, and serial tasks can be determined. Even in joint undertakings, work assignments are distributed on an individual basis; each man's expected contribution is made known to him and he is held accountable for it. Tasks, of course, vary in complexity and duration, and in the frequency of and susceptibility to review. But again, as in the case of competence, machinery exists in a variety of forms for gauging both the desired and undesired contributions of individuals: procedures for setting and measuring production quotas in industry, tissue committees and the performance of post-mortems in hospitals, the rotation of men from assignment to assignment in a variety of military and civil service jobs, to name just a few. Moreover, many arrangements designed to measure competence also provide evidence for ascertaining accountability.

The principle of individual accountability pertains not only to men's occupational pursuits but also to their relationship to legal institutions. Persons who have committed infractions of the law (other than minor and numerically frequent offenses, such as traffic violations) are subjected to inquiries to determine the extent of their responsibility; that is, to discover if there were extenuating circumstances: could the individual tell right from wrong, were his actions affected by mental illness, would he have committed the same act "with a policeman at his elbow," had he the capacity to exercise good judgment? Settling the legal question of guilt or innocence requires an assessment of premeditation and an indication of whether the individual had sufficient control over himself and his circumstances at the time of the offense so that he could have elected not to do what he did. In other words, the impact of all forces beyond his control is subtracted, leaving a residue of individual accountability.

Punishments for criminal offenses are usually fixed according to rules within the legal process itself; but where imprisonment is involved, it is often within the power of the prisoner to reduce the length of his sentence by good behavior. With punishments for civil crimes, the offender "holds the jailhouse key in his own hands;" by making restitution he can stay out of jail or get out of jail or avoid the payment of a fine. Thus, the legal system places great emphasis on voluntary individual effort both for getting into jail and getting out. The principle is nicely summed up in the lore of prisoners: "If you can't pull the time, don't pull the crime."

Contractual Affiliation

The fifth characteristic of an industrial labor force is that occupational employment is usually obtained through contractual agreement. The meaning of the term "employment" should not be restricted simply to agreements specifying the nature of the exchange between activities contributed and remuneration received, although this type of agreement constitutes the common form of labor contract known as hiring. More broadly, employment refers to the nature of the affiliation between a person and an occupational position; frequently the affiliation is established with an organization because certain positions do not exist outside of organizational settings. Employment in this sense includes other types of affiliative contracts besides hiring. For example, physicians may be hired by insurance companies or by public health agencies to perform specific and often routine duties. However, as a means of using hospital facilities to treat their own patients, they affiliate themselves with hospitals through the device of "privilege," not by that of hiring. Some lawyers, usually young and inexperienced ones, may be hired by law firms; others practice alone or by joining themselves to a firm by partnership. The variety of affiliative arrangements is large and includes, in addition to those mentioned, conscription, characteristic of membership in the armed forces, and patronage, typically found in the artistic professions and to some extent in the academic.

According to Parsons: *"Contract makes possible the freedom of individuals and collectivities to make ad hoc agreements to exchange goods and money, and to enter into mutual obligations involving future performances."* [16] Although the nature of contract need not be limited to exchanges involving goods and money, its *ad hoc* nature, the specification of terms, the possibilities of bargaining until an agreement is struck, and the definition of limits beyond which the agreement is considered broken are all characteristics of contract that apply centrally to occupational employment.[17] Moreover, contract consists of an impersonal agreement based on specific interests over a stipulated period of time; the parties to it bind themselves only to its terms and do not bind themselves as persons.

Many forms of contractual arrangements are guaranteed by the law of the state. In the purchase of property, for example, legal sanctions apply not only to the breaking of contracts but to entering into them as well. In other forms of contract, administrative rules of organizations apply, rather than laws of the state. Yet these agreements are made workable not by the fear of what may happen if they are broken, but by the good faith and voluntary compliance of the parties involved: by tenants paying their rent, by workers doing their jobs, by lawyers defending their clients and doctors treating their patients without exploiting them. Psychologically, then, contractual agreements require that persons have, besides the willingness to comply, the capacity to trust, and the ability to take into account the interests of the other person.

Banfield, in his poignant description of a small, southern Italian village, finds that most of the peasants he questioned would prefer owning a small plot of land to sharecropping a larger and more profitable one, because ownership, even at a financial sacrifice, eliminates the necessity of making a contract with the owner, an unavoidable and, as it turns out, uncomfortable by-product of sharecropping. *"The gain from the larger holding would [not] offset the burden of having to get along with a landlord. Their [the peasants'] explanations showed how anxiety, suspicion, and hate make cooperation burdensome."* [18] Similarly, the village physician reports that patients he has treated well all of their lives *". . . come to him with the greatest suspicion—as if by coming they were serving his purposes, not theirs—and lie about their symptoms."* [19] Trust, to be sure, is a complex sentiment. One of its components, however, is the capacity to put oneself in another person's position when his circumstances differ from one's own; a second is the capacity to understand that a complementary agreement can be reached at the intersection of distinct and specific interests; a third is the capacity to yield in one's self-interest in order to advance the joint or collective interest. The viability of contract as an institutional form depends on the widespread distribution of these psychological capacities in a population, capacities closely tied to the norms of universalism and specificity.

The existence of an industrial occupational system implies the availability not only of persons with the psychological capacities appropriate for holding jobs and coping with the demands they create, but also of those with the capacities that enable them to deal with others in *their* occupational pursuits; in fact, many of the capacities in question are the same. The carpenters, teachers, policemen, lathe operators, newspaper reporters, and stock brokers of society are also the customers, patients, depositors, renters, and litigants of society, these being some of the client statuses that mark the boundary between the occupational and nonoccupational worlds. While most jobs require some previous training, people carry on client activities with little or no formal training. Experience, both direct and indirect, teaches the complex activities involved in being a patient, a litigant, or a student. Some client activities appear so elementary as to put no demands on personal capacities, to require no learning at all. But consider the ostensibly undemanding act of riding a bus when the passenger is an immigrant and strange to the customs of his new country:

> [*Israeli*] *bus drivers were observed trying to persuade immigrant passengers that the cost of a ride on one bus was the same as the cost on the bus that had just gone by, or that the driver did not personally profit from each fare he collected, or that the decision for the bus to leave the terminal was not his.*[20]

That is, it was necessary to teach people that the proper standard for conduct in this situation did not require that they protect their self-respect by bargaining over the price, that the activity was standardized, not dependent on the personal whim of the parties involved, and that the procedure was not designed for the personal enrichment of the driver. Parenthetically, it is noteworthy also that Israeli bus drivers as teachers attempted to establish more personalized relationships with immigrants than with regular customers, the better to establish the sense of trust conducive to successful instruction. This is analogous to the creation of goodwill in classrooms, discussed earlier.

The same principle involved in acting as a passenger on a bus underlies all relationships involving persons who engage in occupational pursuits and those who deal with others in their occupational capacities. Thus, if physicians concern themselves primarily with the nature of patients' illnesses, storekeepers with products and customers' ability to pay, bankers with the size of the depositors' balance, treating alike all whose circumstances are alike, then the clients of each must be willing to acknowledge the appropriateness of the treatment they receive and to participate in the relationship in a way that permits the accomplishment of the task at hand. That is to say, there must be at least minimal agreement from both sides on the premises governing the relationship and a willingness to engage in the activities required by those premises.

I have made no attempt here to describe every important facet of an industrial occupational work force, but rather to select properties both significant and characteristic, those typically absent in the economies of preliterate and peasant societies. I have attempted, however, to deal with those aspects of occupational life to which schooling is directly related. One possible danger in doing this is to select so adroitly that the chance of not finding a connection between occupation and schooling becomes foreclosed. However, there are protections against such stacking of the cards: to draw the description of occupational life from sources not concerned with the relationship between occupation and schooling, and to search for those characteristics of the occupational system widely acknowledged to be central and distinguishing.[21]

The separation of the workplace from the household is perhaps the most important of the five characteristics of an industrial work force. In an economy in which the production of goods and services for a relatively free market has great priority, the performance of tasks required by the productive process will increase in importance relative to the maintenance of loyalty among kin. Isolating work from the household, then, frees men from these loyalties, removes them from a setting in which they are entitled to special treatment that may interfere with their performance of market- or client-oriented tasks, and permits the selection of workers according to the relevance and proficiency of their contributions rather than to other considerations. *In terms of the requirements of the productive processes,* the separation of the workplace has a liberating effect: it frees men from a setting whose members are bound in relationships of diffuse solidarity, whose status and support are guaranteed even if they fail to contribute to the best of their ability, and whose conduct toward each other is governed more by the particularities of paired relationships than by standards applicable to classes of membership and types of situations; it frees them from the claims that arise in a setting in which conduct follows the principles of diffuseness, dependence, ascription, and particularism.

Given the separation of work and household, the nature of occupational life is determined largely by the characteristics of the workplace, among the most important of which is the distinction between the occupational position and the worker as a person. The significance of this distinction lies in the fact that a worker occupies a position primarily by virtue of possessing specific capacities related to the tasks he must perform, whatever other capacities he may possess, and that any individual possessing them is eligible to fill the position. Occupational employment, therefore, follows the principles of specificity and universalism, principles consistent with the demands of modern production and technology, of organizational and professional authority, and with the extensive prevalence of job mobility characteristic of a free labor market. Given the cluster of tasks and activities associated with occupational positions, the conduct of workers is judged according to the competence of their individual performance; that is, according to the norms of achievement and independence:

The organizations for formal instruction are charged with qualifying people for work and allocating them to an ever wider spectrum of job specialties. They thus come under heavy pressure to be continually oriented to the provision of expert labor . . . as a rapidly changing technology makes obsolescent old skills and jobs and new demands on competence. With this, education becomes more a part of the economic order than ever before.[22]

The allocative function of schools, of course, is familiar enough. Qualifying people for work, however, involves much more than training competence in job-related skills; it involves as well the shaping of men's states of mind, and gaining their willingness to accept standards of conduct related to holding a job as well as to master its component activities.

THE POLITICAL WORLD

The impact of schooling on the political aspects of public life— citizenship, in the more usual construction of that term—remains very much an open question. Traditionally, the schools have offered pupils a political diet of courses in civics, citizenship, and problems of democracy (for the most part bowdlerized versions of enlightenment philosophy), courses whose titles have already become pejorative. Underlying the school's political curriculum has been the assumption that the functioning of a democratic polity requires an active, literate, and informed electorate. Observers of political life have long noted the relationship between the number of years people have attended school and the nature of their political behavior. Questions about the number of years spent in schools are staples of political surveys, and there is evidence that literacy, voting, tolerance, and political interest and participation are all related to schooling; yet the political meaning of school attendance and the nature of its relationship to democracy remain elusive.

The complexity of this relationship between education and polity appears in Lipset's demonstration that literacy rates vary with form of government. In comparing thirteen stable European and English-speaking democracies, seventeen European dictatorships and unstable democracies, seven Latin American democracies and unstable dictatorships, and thirteen stable Latin American dictatorships he finds that the percentages of literate persons in the population, averaged across each group of nations, rank respectively as follows: 96%, 85%, 74%, 46%.[23] The interpretation of these findings remains far from unequivocal, even though the expected association between literacy and democracy does appear. First, although the stable Anglo-European democracies have higher rates of literacy than the European dictatorships, their rates are not much higher; both sets of European countries have exceedingly high rates. Among the dictatorships, however, there appear to be more countries with large nonindustrial sectors than among the democracies; thus the relationship between literacy and polity might be confounded somewhat by the association between literacy and economy, at least for this group of European nations. High rates of literacy, that is, might prevail in either democratic or totalitarian states if they are equally industrialized. Second, the classification of countries mixes stable and unstable governments, and the relationship between stability and literacy differs in the two large world regions, Europe and Latin America. The particular difficulty in interpreting the data does, however, suggest that the relevance of schooling to politics might be found in the nature of major social institutions and the relationships among them.

Eckstein has argued that for governments to be stable there must be similarities, or at least common elements, in the authority structures of major institutions arrayed in terms of their closeness to government.[24] *"We have every reason to think,"* he states, *"that economic organizations cannot be organized in a truly democratic manner, at any rate not without consequences that no one wants."*[25] The same is true of the organization of families. If, however, there is a gradient in the characteristics of authority patterns, or what seems more likely, important common elements in these patterns between adjacent social institutions, the likelihood of governmental stability increases. A theoretical proposition of this kind might help to interpret the empirical findings reported by Lipset, yet there remains the prior task of describing the nature of the polity before such common elements can be discovered.

If the occupational system involves the mobilization of effort for the production of goods and services in industrial societies, the political system represents the means for expressing and mobilizing the variety of interests found in a population and for binding the members in support of governmental policies. Three types of political system predominate in modern nations: two-party democracies, such as the United States and Great Britain; multi-party states, more or less democratic or alternately democratic and authoritarian, such as France and Italy; and totalitarian nations, such as the Soviet Union and other Eastern European countries within its sphere. In multi-party systems, sharply divided interests find organized political expression through parties. Commenting on France, Lipset notes: *"For many decades it has been divided between clericals and anti-clericals, supporters and opponents of a planned economy, and supporters and opponents of parlimentary government, with a few rural-urban cleavages as well."* [26] The party system remains unstable in part because of the failure to resolve cleavages going back in time to the Revolution, because of a two-ballot (run-off) electoral system, and because of the absence until recently of a strong presidential system. The resolution of certain basic conflicting interests in such systems must characteristically await the formation of a coalition government *following* an election, a solution well known for its long-run instability.

In totalitarian states, a single party takes precedence, its purpose not to gain electoral victory, but to mobilize the energies of the people behind the goals of the state, *". . . to organize all the activities of the individual (work, sport, amusements, leisure, culture, and family life) and to extend beyond the purely political domain."* [27] The resolution of conflicting interests must occur within the apparatus of the party itself.

I am concerned here, however, not with the whole range of political structures found in modern industrial nations but with the American two-party democracy; the nature of the demands, constraints, and opportunities it presents to members of the electorate; and certain of the psychological capacities relevant for coping with those demands, constraints, and opportunities. The dominant characteristics of this type of political system can be discovered in the nature of (1) the electoral process, (2) the parties and political coalitions, and (3) the character of office-holding and succession.

Electoral Process

At the national level, each party in a two-party system seeks electoral victory by gaining majority support for a presidential candidate. But if such a system is to continue beyond a few elections (that is, not become either a one- or multi-party system) a victorious party can neither capture the political machinery of the state and drive the opposition into submission nor tolerate its own dissolution into warring factions unable to unite behind a candidate. It must, in other words, continually seek the support of a broad constituency but at the same time not mobilize that constituency in pursuit of the permanent capture of power. In a country as diverse as the United States, with its conflicting interests based on social class, occupation, ethnicity, race, religion, region, urban and nonurban residence, union membership, and so forth, parties, to gain the majority necessary for electoral victory, must cast a wide net. *"Elections,"* Lipset observes, *"become occasions for seeking the broadest possible base of support by convincing divergent groups of their common interests."* [28] Victory at the polls carries obvious advantages to candidates and party officials; to members of the electorate who support the winner, it brings the prospect of a national administration whose programs of legislation and foreign policy appear more likely to advance their interests than does the program of the opposition. In fact, it is this prospect that makes it possible for members of an electorate to compress widely divergent interests into at least temporary support for one of only two party programs and candidates.

Times change, however; people's circumstances (particularly economic and residential) change, national administrations keep their promises with more or less fidelity, the content of issues changes, national and international events call for responses unanticipated at the time of election, and the composition of the electorate itself changes as new groups of young people reach voting age and old people die. In other words, prevailing conditions favor party realignments, but to be politically successful, any new realignment must still embrace a broad spectrum of interests. The contrast with multi-party systems is clear: in such systems, *"Parties do not hope to gain a majority, they usually seek to win the greatest possible electoral support from a limited base. They therefore stress the interests of that base and the cleavages which set it apart from other groups in society."* [29] The effects are often divisive enough to produce volatile coalition governments and to invite the appearance of centralized and autocratic governments to rescue a nation from the grip of its own political instability.

In two-party democracies, the implication of the electoral system for political parties is clear. Parties must encompass broad coalitions of people representing diverse interests; they must be fluid in their membership and generally nonideological in their appeals for support. The population of our nation contains diverse rather than polarized social and economic interests, and men can be pulled in several different political directions depending on the roles they play—as workers, as city dwellers, as union members, as Negroes, as Catholics, and so on. But they can express themselves politically by voting for one of two candidates, and so the major political parties must encompass within themselves almost the full range of political sentiment, from left to right, represented in the country. Although the two main American parties differ consistently on left and right issues, they don't differ by very much; in fact, they resemble each other in composition, and each contains within it the main factions of *national* political cleavage;[30] they resolve conflicting interests, at least temporarily, through primary elections and through the nomination process within each party *prior to* national elections. Moreover, since elections are decided on the basis of a simple majority of those voting rather than by a run-off, voters are usually reluctant to "waste" a vote on a third party candidate. This forces those with dissident political impulses to remain within the two-party structure with the result that both parties retain a diversity of political sentiment within them.[31]

A party structure of this nature puts certain demands on party officials and candidates, on the one hand, and members of the electorate, on the other. The task of party leaders, particularly during the period before an election, is to attract and retain those most marginally committed to the party and its candidate. Key, for example, describes how in 1960 Kennedy could count on the continued support of Catholic Democrats but feared the defection of Protestant Democrats. His strategy was to reach these potential defectors with an appeal to party loyalty in the hope that it would override the prevailing religious antagonism against a Catholic presidential candidate.[32] The appeal might be a global one to party loyalty, as in this case, or it might be narrowly directed to a specific interest (such as farm price supports, civil rights legislation, etc.) designed to attract the support of some interest group without at the same time driving out some other group already marginally lined up.

Parties and Coalitions

The American voter governs his political behavior within the framework of the party system, and most voters identify themselves predominantly with one party at the national level. *"In all successful democracies,"* Galbraith reminds us facetiously, *"the vast majority of people, including those who speak with the greatest passion, get their political affiliations not by ratiocination but by inheritance. To know how people will vote, you have only to know how their grandparents voted in the male line."*[33] While there is no need to accept this hyperbole at face value, the fact of stable party com-

SCHOOLING, WORK, AND POLITICS

mitment has been well documented. Yet at the same time there is much ticket-splitting, party-switching from one election to the next, and abstaining from the polls, much of which can be attributed to the demands that this type of party system makes on the electorate.

The capacity of members of the electorate to collaborate, to strike political bargains, and to avoid combining into exclusive and hostile camps is one of the hallmarks of democratic polities.[34] Key informs us:

> The American is said to be politically pragmatic. Hence, his responses to public issues are not fixed in advance by a rigid pattern of belief that produces predictable and firmly held positions on most public questions. Rather, the predominant set of attitudes predisposes the public to judge each question as it arises on its merits and thereby enables men of good will to arrive at a solution de novo as the situation demands.[35]

Many observers have noted that the diversity of organized interests characteristic of democratic nations requires that many members of the electorate affiliate themselves with groups whose political positions on various issues differ, with the result that these members have both multiple and conflicting affiliations. If one's ethnic or religious identifications predispose to voting one way and one's occupational memberships predispose to voting another, the resulting pressures militate toward a personal resolution of the conflict. One form of resolution is a reduction of the emotional involvement and political passion that people invest in support of their various interests. The greater the number of inconsistent pressures on individuals, the more difficult it becomes for them to adopt a strongly held and ideologically consistent posture in their political conduct; likewise, the greater the opportunities to compare one political stance with another and to ally with others who hold differing views in support of a candidate or an issue. Thus the Protestant worker or wheat farmer in 1960, whose pocketbook may have predisposed him to vote Democratic, would have to weigh economic interest against religious interest. The important point, however, is that in such internal conflicts of interest, there is a real contest; people do go one way or the other yet without feeling that they have seriously compromised a principle. Similarly, when an individual's interests accumulate and reinforce each other in a consistent direction, the potentiality for compromise, for joining with strange bedfellows, and for entering alliances decreases, because compromising more closely approximates a threat to principle.

Traditionally, interests tied to membership in the family and in the church have been among the most difficult to reconcile with the demands of political give-and-take. *"Religious differences,"* Key tells us, *"seem not to be susceptible to compromise; rather, men are disposed to torture each other in the name of God when they dispute questions of religion,"*[36] unless, that is, a free religious tradition removes matters of faith and doctrine from the arena of political controversy and bargaining. The connection between the functioning of a democratic polity and the cooling of religious convictions is ingeniously illustrated by Almond and Verba. Their American, British, German, Italian, and Mexican respondents were asked how they would feel about the marriage of a son or daughter to a member of an opposing political party. They found that preferences for the spouse to be of the same political persuasion were most prevalent in Italy and Germany, where one of the major parties— the Christian Democrats in both countries—is church-connected. Not surprisingly, these two nations, with difficult-to-resolve ideological positions built into party conflict (and on other bases beside religion), have endured considerable political instability over the past 50 years, and both have resorted to strongly authoritarian governments during this period as a means of resolving highly divisive tensions. In the two democratic nations, the United States and Britain, there is overwhelming indifference within the population to the political persuasion of the prospective spouse of one's children.[37] While Americans and Englishmen might balk at the prospects of religious intermarriage, a cross-party intermarriage does not raise this problem, because party identifications are far more independent of religious persuasion than they are in Italy and Germany.

Many observers have emphasized the importance of the family as the prime unit of *party* identification in democracies. According to Greenstein: *"Party identifications probably develop without much explicit teaching on the part of parents, more or less in the form of a gradual awareness by the child of something which is part of him. The process doubtless is similar to the development of ethnic and religious identifications."*[38] Moreover, evidence suggests that party identification is learned young, evidently prior to the time that children orient themselves politically to issues: *"The prevalence of party identifications among nine-year olds is especially striking when we realize that the proportion of adult Americans who identify with parties (75%) is not much greater."*[39] This is not to say that all members of the same family vote alike, but it does mean that the members of a family are likely to show considerable consistency in party affiliation in any one generation and across generations. Families, that is, support a political entity—the party—which contains a broad range of interests, one that cuts across the major lines of social cleavage, and one with which people seem to identify in a general way before they can distinguish among substantive political issues; they do not tend to line up along the main lines of cleavage.

Office-Holding and Succession

Holding political office in a democratic nation, either by election or appointment, is very much like holding a job. According to Bendix:

Persons who occupy positions of authority are not personal rulers, but superiors who temporarily occupy an office by virtue of which they possess limited authority. As a result the officials are appointed on the basis of contracts, their loyalty is enlisted in order to ensure the faithful execution of their official duties, and their work is rewarded by a regular salary and by prospects of regular advancement in a lifetime career.[40]

Election to office, of course, carries no guarantee of a continuing career; in fact, the career is limited by a clear definition of the total term of office. Moreover, election is not contractual in the sense that employment is, though metaphorically there is a form of contract that the candidate and officeholder enters into with his electoral constituency, not with employing or appointing superiors. Beyond these differences, however, there is a clear definition of office and of the limits of authority. The right of officials to exercise authority derives from the fact that the government in power is legally constituted and that they exercise it impartially in only those classes of situations that are defined by legislation and precedent.

One of the hallmarks of modern governments is the existence of a civil service which is tolerably neutral, in that competent performance of tasks assigned to functionaries has a higher priority than party allegiance, and neutral in that government agencies are expected to provide equitable and impartial services to citizens of the nation. By implication, the average citizen must know how to recognize an equitable service when he sees one and how to participate in relationships with public officials in which he is treated like everyone else in the same circumstances. In the more democratic societies, as Almond and Verba observe, members of the citizenry tend in fact to acknowledge that they receive equitable treatment by government officials. In reply to questions about whether they are treated "as well as anyone else" by police and by government housing and tax agents, Americans and British report overwhelmingly that they expect such treatment (between 80% and 90% of respondents), while among Germans, Italians, and Mexicans markedly smaller proportions expect fair treatment (between 30% and 75% across those three countries).[41]

One of the prime distinguishing characteristics of democratic polities is their solution to the problem of succession in office. Legitimate procedures exist for filling and vacating political offices, and office-holders and their supporters are willing to acknowledge their obligation to relinquish office at the conclusion of its term, as well as to honor the rightful claims of political opponents to hold office. Voluntary yielding of the powers and perquisites of office is not to be taken for granted, since other ways of filling and vacating offices prevail in other political systems. For example, revenge and *coup d'état* are the political way of life in more than a few nations, both representing a mode of political operation in which the office becomes either a personal extension of the man or an agency for the expression of one particular ideological position to the exclusion of all others. It is not so much the problem of legitimate succession that must be solved in democracies—monarchies also provide for this—but that of legitimate, frequent, and periodic turnover in office, a process that depends on a mutual trust between the parties that the other will neither usurp the machinery of government nor institute a different kind of regime. Whatever else they disagree on, the parties in a democratic polity must at least agree on the nature of the regime.

Election to political office is an achievement, the outcome of having successfully nourished and mobilized popular support behind a candidacy; continuation in office and reelection similarly represent the achievement of having maintained popular backing. The whole process is costly, not only in money, but in commitments made to people and groups (promissory notes on which one must deliver) and in compromises. Electoral defeat, especially for an incumbent, represents a kind of failure involving the acknowledgment of political weakness and loss of power to which the appropriate response is graceful acceptance and a consideration of the possibilities of running again. The loss, however, is not merely a personal one, nor is it trivial; since a candidate's backers go down with him, it is collective. For the supporters of a candidate, the sense of defeat is not as direct but consists rather in the acknowledgment that the man they backed to advance their interests, or at least who they thought would advance them more than the opposition would, will not be empowered to do so. They must then hope for the best from the opposition, which is not too difficult when the opposition does not stand for radically different political, economic, and social principles.

The democratic processes of office-holding and attainment, then, are centrally organized around the principles of achievement and failure. An electoral process so organized puts constraints on both office-holders and candidates to cope with the problems posed by these principles. Success must not be exploited into the aggrandizement of office; defeat must not become desperation so that the fact of loss becomes the occasion for questioning the legitimacy of the principles governing political succession itself. Of course, the fact that the opposition consists largely of people whose political positions on many issues of the day are not too different from one's own makes defeat easier to take. The government does not fall into the hands of mortal political enemies.

Key has stated that within the population of a democratic nation there exists among individuals ". . . *a sensitivity to the problems of the other fellow, a capacity to recognize when it is futile to fight and more sensible to wait, a disposition to seek out areas of agreement and to maximize them, a tendency to sweep conflict under the rug, an unprincipled inclination to split the difference or compromise."* [42] In essence, he has identified a set of habits of mind more conducive to participation in a two-party political system than committed to the uncompromising defense of ideological principle, the imperiousness of political demands, and the sense of personal aggrandizement. The latter is more likely to be associated with multi-party systems with their notoriously unstable coalition governments. This is not to suggest that the habits of mind that Key finds prevalent in democracies are absent in nondemocratic polities; political bargaining occurs to some extent everywhere. The question, however, is where it starts and where it stops.

According to classical liberal political theory, members of the electorate of a democratic state must keep informed on the issues of the day, vote, engage in political discussion, participate actively in campaigns, and adopt a political stance based on principle. Enough has been learned about the actual workings of the democratic political process, however, to question whether the independent citizen contemplated by the classical theory is actually the mainstay of the political system. In fact, his origins seem to lie more in the tenets of the theory than in the actual demands that a democratic system creates for its participants. Scholarly opinion on the political process appears divided in its emphasis; some observers concerned with explaining party preference and the extent of participation and apathy have fastened on voters' responses to group pressures;[43] others, who are concerned more with changes in party preference and less with its content and the degree of participation see the electorate as ". . . *moved by concern about central and relevant questions of public policy, of governmental performance, and of executive personality.*"[44] The polemic of scholarly debate should not conceal the fact that out of research concerned with different but overlapping problems—political preference and change in preference—a rather consistent psychological portrait of the political participant emerges.

According to a variety of sources, the democratic participant appears as more trustful, tolerant, considerate, compromising, and less passionately involved than his counterpart in nondemocratic systems. Almond and Verba state:

In the United States and Britain the belief that people are generally cooperative, trustworthy, and helpful is frequent, and it has political consequences. Belief in the benignity of one's fellow citizen is directly related to one's propensity to join with others in political activity. General social trust is translated into politically relevant trust.[45]

It is also of a piece with the trustfulness that makes contract a viable form of agreement in the marketplace.

My intent here is not to replace a theoretical glorification of the democratic participant with an empirical one; in fact, it is not to glorify at all, but rather to locate those psychological capacities that enable individuals to engage in a form of political life that constrains them to compromise, to form relatively easy coalitions with others who disagree with them, to accept political defeat but to come back another day, to find a reasonable resolution of the conflicting interests related to multiple roles and social identities, and to acknowledge the legitimacy of the opposition's right to rule. Trust, toleration, consideration, and compromise, despite their obvious differences in meaning, all include one common element: the ability to visualize another person's position and circumstances and to see one's own in relation to it; in short, the capacity to empathize that Lerner found necessary for the transition between traditional and modern social existence to occur. In addition to the capacity to empathize, participation in a democratic polity also requires a particular mode of dealing with success and failure: one that allows an individual to tolerate both sets of circumstances without acting to change the regime (the rules of the game) that brought them about; and that allows individuals, acting alone or collectively, to change their circumstances within bounds set by the rules.

The political participant in a two-party democracy must either come to terms with the very small number of real partisan choices he has or drive himself to distraction by weighing a multitude of politically relevant considerations in order to calculate his political preferences; essentially, he can either vote the party or vote the man. He can, of course, abstain or vote for a third-party candidate, but the impact of these alternatives is often more visceral than political in its effect on a two-party system. There is probably no psychologically viable way to express political interest that reflects both the summation of one's positions on the numerous issues of foreign policy, taxation, public welfare, civil rights, farm policy, labor policy, business policy, etc., on the one hand, and on the other, the response to pressures based on religion, status, race, ethnicity, friendship, education, residence, and kinship. Voting the party or the man indicates, however, that individuals have arrived at a political posture, at least temporarily, that *in effect* represents a resolution of conflicting interests based on current issues and social identifications. The capacity to arrive at such a resolution can have at least three origins: first, simply expressing a traditional (family) party preference (voting one's genes) where party preference itself represents a pre-ordered resolution of diverse interests; second, voting a personal preference for a man, which may or may not coincide with traditional party preference, a response psychologically equivalent to the first; and third, actually weighing *specific* interests one against the other (for example, by backing a Democratic candidate for president, thus expressing support for welfare legislation but also acknowledging that his election will require him to pay political debts to Southern segregationists).

To participate in this type of political system, with its two loosely-organized, nonideological parties, one must be able to accept the norms of specificity and universalism. The first enables people to reach a political decision on an issue-by-issue basis rather than as the expression of a deeply-held ideological position; the second enables people to acknowledge that other members of the electorate are in much the same political circumstances as themselves, needing to resolve similarly conflicting interests rather than support sharply opposed values that yield stubbornly if at all to resolution. The political posture of the democratic participant, in other words, is based on the capacity to identify categorically with others in support of and in opposition to a variety of specific issues, with the understanding that others do likewise and thus constitute no serious threat as political opponents. Such a posture is one that permits the formation of loose and undisciplined party coalitions characteristic of the American system. The system's weakness, however, is its difficulty in coping with alien ideological assaults from abroad because of its meagre experience with ideological diversity at home. As Hartz has commented: *"Americans seem to oscillate between fleeing from the rest of the world and embracing it with too ardent a passion. An absolute national morality is inspired either to withdraw from 'alien' things or to transform them: it cannot live in comfort constantly by their side."* [46] Participants in a two-party democratic system have great difficulty in striking bargains with those whose political interests cannot readily be reached through give and take on specific issues:

Where all adults enjoy the rights of citizenship, access to public employment will be unrestricted except for educational qualifications. Similarly, the growth of plebiscitarian politics will give rise to a proliferation of attempts to influence the administration and to a regulariza-

tion of contacts between administrators and the "public." These developments reveal the conditions under which national allegiance grows at the expense of group solidarity. In Western societies, "organized interests" have formed in great numbers on the impersonal basis of common interests. They have been encouraged by the right to form associations, by the administrative use of group representation, by the great resources available at the national level, and by the degree to which politics has become a struggle over the distribution of the national product.[47]

The claims of citizens to special treatment decline according to the extent that their access to the realm of political life becomes universalized, for when citizens join with others in broad and diverse coalitions that include almost the full range of political sentiment to create a government according to the rules of a two-party democratic regime, they thereby relinquish their claim to benefits to which others are not similarly entitled.

EPILOGUE

The objective of socialization is to produce competent people, as competence is defined in any given society. It aims to develop a person who can take care of himself, support others, conceive and raise children, hunt boar or grow vegetables, vote, fill out an application form, drive an auto, and what have you.[48]

As a developmental process, socialization takes place within a variety of social settings, not only during childhood but all through life. Schools are but one type of institution among many that contribute to the process either by formal design or by effect. In some respects, the contribution of schooling closely resembles that of experiences provided by other settings; there is undoubtedly a considerable overlap among all the types of knowledge obtained from school, from members of one's family, from friends, and from exposure to the mass media. And even though these agencies differ in the kinds of knowledge they provide, clearly they are all capable of imparting it. Consider another area of competence: participation in relationships of authority. Here again, several agencies other than the school undoubtedly contribute to the acquisition of relevant capacities, but just as probably, the experiences they provide pertain to different types of authority relationships. The family, for example, although in certain respects prototypical of all subsequent authority relations, probably creates best those capacities that enable people to adapt themselves in situations involving hierarchy of position, inequalities in power, and subordination based on diffuse personal obligations. Adolescent peer groups, by contrast, without hierarchical distinctions based on position, age, generation, and power, probably contribute best to capacities for getting along in situations where authority is based on collective pressure from equals and colleagues. The school is perhaps best designed for learning to participate in authority relationships based on inequalities in specific capacity rather than on diffuse obligation, and on the occupancy of positions linked by contractual or other formally specific agreements. And although other agencies of socialization undoubtedly contribute to the learning of norms, the school, more than others at the same stages of the life cycle, probably makes a greater impact than they do on learning the norms of independence, achievement, universalism, and specificity.

To put the argument in its proper perspective, I have discussed only part of the question of what is learned in school; namely, those social norms whose acquisition seems related to experiences shaped by some of the school's peculiar structural properties rather than by its instructional program. The nature of those experiences appears related to the fact that the school links the family with the public institutions of adult life (especially those organized around occupations and politics) through phases of the life cycle. That is to say, if children were raised mainly within the confines of kinship units and immediate residential communities, their psychological capacities would be better adapted to cope with the demands of family life and with those varieties of economic and political life that can be organized on a kinship basis, as is characteristically the case in primitive and peasant societies. The central question of this book, then, really concerns only that part of the school's total contribution that pertains to the development of those normative psychological capacties that enable people to manage the social demands placed on them when they participate as adults in public institutions outside the orbit of the family.

I have argued, moreover, that schooling, occupation, and politics, at least in the United States, are reasonably well integrated with one another in the sense that related institutions create similar demands on persons who participate in them, that similar psychological capacities prove appropriate to the demands, for example, of both occupational and political involvement, and that the schools contribute to the creation of those capacities.[49] That is not to say that school-developed capacities are necessarily or invariably appropriate to institutional demands. To the extent that the experience of schooling leaves a residue of accumulated frustration among pupils who have consistently failed in their work or who have found the burdens of independence too threatening to their self-esteem, the normative outcomes supposedly derivable from schooling may not appear, and consequently young persons may lack the capacities they need to cope with the demands placed on them. The effectiveness of schooling, of course, as defined in terms of the acquisition of these capacities, is not guaranteed simply by the availability of the school's resources. For example, when the family, because of its own lack of resources, cannot provide adequate support for children as they proceed through school, the institutionally relevant outcomes of schooling are not as likely to appear as when family support is sufficient.

The extent to which schools contribute to the acquisition of capacities ill-adapted to the demands of public institutional life should not be simply regarded as ineffective schooling. There is an ideological issue here as well as a question of the integration of institutions. For some individuals, the irrelevance of schooling to employment, for whatever reason, can mean great personal and family hardship because employment in industrial society is so important in providing a measure of self-respect and economic sustenance. For others, the inappropriateness of schooling leads not so much to the pathologies of unemployability but rather to forms of deviance and alienation that may provide an impetus for *desirable* social change and reform. It should surprise no one that the integration of schooling with occupational and political institutions should contribute to the stability of an industrial society; the prevailing institutions of a society simply cannot be thought away. Yet to observe their existence and integration is not to justify them ideologically.

How can the psychological capacities apparently acquired through schooling—at least the American species of schooling—be related to the demands of occupational and political institutions of modern nations? The answer is complex. Assuming, for example, that the effective operation of a democratic political system requires office holders and members of the electorate to align themselves in broad and loosely organized party coalitions representing a range of political persuasions on current issues, and assuming that a modern, industrial occupational system requires job holders to enter employment contracts, both institutional systems will operate more effectively if the population contains a substantial component of persons who accept the norm of universalism and act according to it *in the political and occupational spheres* than if it contains a preponderance of persons who act according to the norm of particularism. By the "effective operation" of a system, I mean that a particular type of political regime maintains the allegiance of the electorate, that outstanding disputes get settled over the short and moderately long run, that succession in office occurs continuously and without serious disruptions to the regime, and that in organizations designed for the production of goods and services, workers are able to perform their required productive tasks and organizations continue to operate without serious disruption in either the productive process itself or in the work force. The qualification, "in the political and occupational spheres" is important; it refers to the fact that the citizens of a nation should be able to act appropriately to the situation—in this case, according to universalistic principles in political and occupational life, though not, for example, in the context of family life. To say a "substantial component of persons" must accept and act according to the norm is merely a way of acknowledging our ignorance of empirical relationships; we simply do not know what proportion of a nation's population must possess a given set of capacities for its institutions to operate effectively.

It is inconceivable that the widespread acceptance of universalistic norms is a sufficient condition for the functioning of a democratic polity and a modern, industrial economy; moreover, no one has shown this norm to be a necessary condition nor shown it to be unknown in other types of political and economic systems. If school-derived capacities are neither necessary nor sufficient conditions, what can be said about them? Only that they are relevant and appropriate to the demands of institutional life, and such, it seems, they are. The work of society can get done if people are not burdened with psychologically crushing tasks and if the various major institutions of society can draw adequate human resources for their operation. As Blau reminds us:

Particularistic standards typically produce segregating boundaries in the social structure. Thus, the finding that members of various religious denominations in a community think more highly of and are more attracted to co-religionists than persons in other denominations would show that religion is a particularistic standard and also that it promotes social divisions among members of a community.[50]

If the demands of political life, then, require the weakening of such social divisions as they seem to in two-party democracies, clearly the widespread acceptance of particularistic norms would militate against the viability of a political system whose functioning depends on compromise and the formation of broad nonideological coalitions. Necessary conditions are simply those representing capacities appropriate to demands, whatever the form of those capacities happens to be. The acceptance of particularistic norms would seem to be inappropriate, but there may well be suitable alternatives to universalism. A similar argument, of course, would obtain for other institutional demands in addition to the political and for each of the other norms besides universalism. Whether the particular norms I have discussed here also support other economic and political systems is beside the point, and whether each system has a unique set of conditions remains an empirical question. It is unlikely that any particular capacity, if considered in isolation from other capacities and social conditions, can be understood as a necessary condition of institutional functioning. Necessary conditions are more apt to be found in clusters than one at a time, if for no other reason than the fact that types of political and economic systems can to some extent vary independently of each other.

If the contribution of schooling to democratic political life lies in pupils' acceptance of specific and universalistic norms (among others), then, ironically, it would appear that the more bureaucratic properties of school organization (i.e., those that contribute to pupils' capacities to form transient social relationships, submerge much of their personal identity, and accept the legitimacy of categorical treatment), are most relevant to the creation of a democratic electorate and to the maintenance of a democratic polity. The relevance of these norms to the demands of occupational life have long been acknowledged. If such a conclusion appears ideologically distasteful, it should also be remembered that the same norms seem to contribute also to a sense of tolerance, fairness, consideration, and trustfulness, and to the expectation among members of the populace that they possess a legitimate claim to participate in all areas of public life and that none shall be entitled to special treatment of whatever kind—expectations whose prevalence today underlie some of the more radical social changes that have taken place in American history.

NOTES AND REFERENCES

1.   Edward A. Shils, "Toward a Modern Intellectual Community in the New States," in James S. Coleman (ed.), *Education and Political Development,* p. 498, Princeton University Press, Princeton (1965).

2.   Bernard Berelson, Paul F. Lazarsfeld, and William N. McPhee, *Voting,* p. 314, University of Chicago Press, Chicago (1954); also Seymour M. Lipset, *Political Man,* pp. 216–219, Doubleday, New York (1959).

3.   Clark Kerr, John T. Dunlop, Frederick Harbison, and Charles A. Myers, *Industrialism and Industrial Man,* p. 26, Harvard University Press, Cambridge (1960).

4.   Manning Nash, *Primitive and Peasant Economic Systems,* p. 21, Chandler, San Francisco (1966).

5.   Talcott Parsons, "Some Reflections on the Institutional Framework of Economic Development," in *Structure and Process in Modern Societies,* p. 110, Free Press of Glencoe, New York (1963). The separation of occupation and household is further elaborated by Fallers. "While handicrafts [in peasant societies] may reach extremely high levels of skill and aesthetic expressiveness, and trade may become an important calling, they remain essentially domestic occupations, carried out in the context of the household of the practitioner or his elite patron. . . . Even government is commonly carried out in a domestic idiom, the polity being treated rather like an extension of the ruler's household and public officials his domestic servants. Lacking are those functionally specialized political and economic organizations, so characteristic of modern societies, that are separated from the households of

their members and in which the latter play purely occupational roles in exchange for basic income." Lloyd Fallers, "Equality, Modernity, and Democracy in the New States," in Clifford Geertz (ed.), *Old Societies and New States*, pp. 170–171, Free Press of Glencoe, New York (1963).

6. William G. Buss, "The Massachusetts Conflict-of-Interest Statute: An Analysis," *Boston University Law Review* **45**, No. 3, 353, (1965).

7. For a discussion of the succession of charismatic leaders, see Max Weber, *The Theory of Social and Economic Organization*, translated by A. M. Henderson and Talcott Parsons, pp. 363–386, Oxford University Press, New York (1947): especially the section on the routinization of charisma.

8. Chester I. Barnard, *The Functions of the Executive*, p. 77, Harvard University Press, Cambridge (1956). Barnard clarifies his terminological distinctions as follows: "I shall use the more awkward plan of substituting 'contributors' for 'members' and 'contributions' for the activities constituting organization; but it should be noted that 'contributors,' though including those whom we would ordinarily call 'members' of an organization, is a broader term and may also include others; and that 'contributions' is correspondingly a broader term than 'membership' or 'membership activities.'" *Ibid.*, p. 75.

9. Chester I. Barnard, *ibid.*, p. 139.

10. U.S. Bureau of the Census, *Statistical Abstract of the United States: 1965*. (86th edition.) Table No. 314, p. 228, U.S. Government Printing Office, Washington, D.C. (1965).

11. For a more detailed elaboration of the distinction between the technical and managerial levels of organizations, see Talcott Parsons, "Some Ingredients of a General Theory of Formal Organization," *op. cit.*, pp. 60–64.

12. Lyle Saunders, "Healing Ways in the Spanish Southwest," in E. Gartly Jaco (ed.), *Patients, Physicians, and Illness*, p. 205, Free Press, Glencoe, Ill. (1958).

13. See, for example, the account of informal accomodation between prisoners and guards in Gresham Sykes, *The Society of Captives*, pp. 40–62, Princeton University Press, Princeton (1958); and the account of informal yet proscribed consultation between agents in an office of the Internal Revenue Service reported in

Peter M. Blau, *Dynamics of Bureaucracy,* revised edition, pp. 121–143, University of Chicago Press, Chicago (1963).

14. There are, of course, many qualifications to this contention, depending on the existence of trade unions, seniority provisions, and the like.

15. William Martin, "Preferences for Types of Patients," in Robert K. Merton, George G. Reader, and Patricia L. Kendall (eds.), *The Student Physician,* pp. 196–202, Harvard University Press, Cambridge (1957).

16. Talcott Parsons, "Some Principal Characteristics of Industrial Societies," *op. cit.,* p. 144.

17. Despite their general sociological importance, questions concerning the noncontractual elements of contracts (those aspects not negotiable on an *ad hoc* basis), are not relevant to this discussion. For a full discussion of the noncontractual elements, see Talcott Parsons, *The Structure of Social Action,* pp. 311–314, Free Press, Glencoe, Ill. (1949).

18. Edward C. Banfield, *The Moral Basis of a Backward Society,* p. 91, Free Press of Glencoe, New York (1967).

19. Edward C. Banfield, *ibid.,* p. 119. "They are so suspicious that if I were to visit them professionally and give them something, they would begin to wonder just how much the government is paying me that I can afford to come to their houses and give things away." *Ibid.,* p. 120.

20. Elihu Katz and S. N. Eisenstadt, "Some Sociological Observations on the Response of Israeli Organizations to New Immigrants," *Administrative Science Quarterly* **5,** No. 1, 125 (1960). The permission of Elihu Katz to quote from his paper is gratefully acknowledged.

21. Moreover, this discussion does not involve the empirical testing of hypotheses but rather the statement of a theoretical argument which can later be put to the test.

22. Burton R. Clark, "Interorganizational Patterns of Education," *Administrative Science Quarterly* **10,** No. 2, 226 (1965).

23. Seymour M. Lipset, *op. cit.,* p. 53. He goes on to show that enrollments in primary, secondary, and higher education per 1000 population rank in the same order as literacy.

24. "One must think of societies as being composed of segments which are more or less distant from government. Governments themselves are adult structures, and for this reason families, for example, are more 'vertically' distant from them, in terms of age levels, than schools, and schools more distant from them than purely adult structure. . . . Parties, for example, ordinarily are situated closer to government than pressure groups; among pressure groups certain types may be particularly closely involved in government or parties; and all pressure groups are located more closely to government than non-political organizations [such as the economic or military]." Harry Eckstein, "A Theory of Stable Democracy," p. 10, Center of International Studies, Princeton University, Princeton (1961).

25. Harry Eckstein, *ibid.*, p. 9.

26. Seymour M. Lipset, *The First New Nation,* p. 296, Basic Books, New York (1963). In contrast to France, Kornhauser, in describing the American case, states that: ". . . extensive *cross-cutting solidarities* favor a high level of freedom and consensus: these solidarities help prevent one line of social cleavage from becoming dominant, and they constrain associations to respect the various affiliations of their members lest they alienate them." William Kornhauser, *The Politics of Mass Society,* p. 80, Free Press of Glencoe, New York (1959).

27. Maurice Duverger, *Political Parties,* p. 117, John Wiley and Sons, New York (1963).

28. Seymour M. Lipset, *The First New Nation,* p. 307.

29. Seymour M. Lipset, *ibid.,* p. 307.

30. See Samuel Lubell, *The Future of American Politics,* Harper and Bros., New York (1951), for a discussion of the composition of Democratic and Republican coalitions and the range of groups within each of them.

31. It is noteworthy that during the 1932 and 1936 Depression elections in which, at least according to Marxist doctrine, the greatest incentive to vote for an ideologically left-wing party was present, over 95% of the electorate voted either Democratic or Republican.

32. V. O. Key, *The Responsible Electorate,* pp. 121–122, Harvard University Press, Cambridge (1966).

33.   John K. Galbraith, *The Scotch,* p. 70, Houghton Mifflin, Boston (1964).

34.   Gabriel A. Almond and Sidney Verba, *The Civic Culture,* pp. 123–160, 400–401, Princeton University Press, Princeton (1963).

35.   V. O. Key, *Public Opinion and American Democracy,* p. 49, Alfred A. Knopf, New York (1965).

36.   V. O. Key, *ibid.,* p. 40.

37.   Gabriel A. Almond and Sidney Verba, *op. cit.,* pp. 132–143. The Mexican situation is more like the American and British than like the German and Italian, perhaps, as Almond and Verba suggest, because there has been a *modus vivendi* reached between the state and the church.

38.   Fred I. Greenstein, *Children and Politics,* p. 73, Yale University Press, New Haven (1965).

39.   Fred I. Greenstein, *ibid.,* pp. 71–72.

40.   Reinhard Bendix, *Nation-Building and Citizenship,* p. 161, John Wiley and Sons, New York (1964).

41.   Gabriel A. Almond and Sidney Verba, *op. cit.,* p. 108.

42.   V. O. Key, *Public Opinion and American Democracy,* pp. 51–52.

43.   See in particular Paul F. Lazarsfeld, Bernard Berelson, and Hazel Gaudet, *The People's Choice,* Columbia University Press, New York (1948); and Berelson, Lazarsfeld, and William N. McPhee, *Voting.* Key speaks somewhat disparagingly of this approach, stating: "Nor does a heroic conception of the voter emerge from the new analyses of electoral behavior. They can be added up to a conception of voting not as a civic decision but as an almost purely deterministic act. Given knowledge of certain characteristics of a voter—his occupation, his residence, his religion, his national origin, and perhaps certain of his attitudes—one can predict with a high probability the direction of his vote." V. O. Key, *The Responsible Electorate,* p. 5.

44.   V. O. Key, *ibid.,* pp. 7–8.

45.   Gabriel A. Almond and Sidney Verba, *op. cit.,* p. 285. These writers also report that Americans and British mention generosity and considerateness as qualities they admire most in people more frequently than Germans, Italians, and Mexicans (59%, 65%, 42%, 25%, and 36%, respectively), *ibid.,* pp. 265–266.

46.   Louis Hartz, *The Liberal Tradition in America,* p. 286, Harcourt, Brace, New York (1955).

47. Reinhard Bendix, *op. cit.*, pp. 141–142.

48. Alex Inkeles, "Social Structure and the Socialization of Competence," *Harvard Educational Review* **36**, No. 3, 265 (1966).

49. Concerning the integration of institutions, Eckstein comments: ". . . one can . . . speak meaningfully of a congruence of authority patterns if the patterns have a certain 'fit' with one another—if they dovetail with, or support, the governmental pattern, however indirectly. One way in which they can do this is by the partial imitation of the governmental authority patterns in other social structures. Democratic (or other) pretenses, if taken seriously and carried far, may have important consequences for the operation of the governmental structure, even though they are pretenses. Furthermore, structures like economic or military organizations may, in some cases, willingly incur certain functional disadvantages for the sake of acting out norms associated with governments in their substantive decision-making processes." Harry Eckstein, *op. cit.*, p. 9.

50. Peter M. Blau, "Operationalizing a Conceptual Scheme: The Universalism-Particularism Pattern Variable," *American Sociological Review* **27**, No. 2, 166 (1962).

AUTHOR INDEX

SUBJECT INDEX

Empathy in industrial societies, 104, 126–127, 139, 141
Employment, 16, 64, 96, 145
Equity (or fairness), 14, 74, 79–84, 148
Ethnicity, ethnic group membership, 13, 78, 107, 135
Expertise, 119
Extracurricular activities, 72–73

Families
  age composition of, 14
  children leaving, 10, 31
  continuing membership in, 2, 9, 20, 35
  and continuing support for a career, 96
  duration of membership in, 9
  emotional bonds within, 21, 29, 96
  equity within, 22, 76, 80–82
  instruction within, 31, 43
  nuclear and conjugal compared, 11, 25
  personal attributes of members of, 17, 18, 80
  rewards and punishments in, 14, 34, 35
  sequence of events in, 11, 31, 83
  sex differences within, 14, 17
  size of, 8
  visibility within, 19, 20, 79

Goodwill, creation of, 35, 37, 128
Grades (and marking), 19, 34–35, 36, 82
Guidance services, 18, 33

Ideology, 28, 74, 85, 145
Independence, norm of, 66–70, 123–125, 129, 144
Industrial societies
  adult occupational status within, 95, 96, 114–130
  characteristic demands of, 94, 145–148
  characteristics of the labor force in, 114–128
  citizenship within, 101, 106, 109
  client relationships within, 127–128
  distinction between persons and position in, 78, 112, 117–118
  and empathy, 104, 126–127, 139, 141
  and investment in education, 95
  legal accountability within, 124–125
  normative principles of occupations within, 95–97
  and occupational failure, 72, 145
  presence of a middle class in, 97–98

public welfare and universalistic groupings in, 116
  schooling as transitional within, 84, 91, 94, 108–109
  schooling specific to, 2, 5–6
  specialized positions within, 64, 124
Instruction, 5, 7, 20, 32, 33, 42, 55, 92
Internalization versus acceptance of norms, 45

Language of children, 53–55
Legal institutions, 124
Legitimacy, 119, 137
Life cycle, stages in the, 2, 144

Mass media, 65, 143
Medical institutions, 121, 125

National political regime, 98, 138
National tradition, values, and unity, 2, 42, 85
Neighborhood characteristics
  ethnic, 9, 13
  religious, 9, 13
  social class, 9, 13, 21
Nongraded classes, 14
Norms
  acceptance of, 44, 55, 93
  of achievement, 47, 70–73, 83, 118, 129, 139, 144
  and behavior distinguished, 29
  changes in, 47–48, 49–51
  conformity to and deviance from, 45
  defined, 44, 63
  generalization of, 50–51
  of independence, 66–70, 123–125, 129, 144
  intensity of, 45
  internalization versus acceptance of, 45
  situational effects upon, 52, 55, 144
  of specificity, 74–84, 127–129, 142, 144
  of universalism, 74–84, 127, 129, 142, 144, 146
  and values distinguished, 45
  verbal expression and the learning of, 53

Occupations
  affiliation with, 117–118, 125–127
  apprenticeship for, 66
  independent of the family, 115–116
  and individual accountability, 64, 69, 123–125